Domestic Planner® Systems

Domestic Planner® Systems

By Diana Koenig

Domestic Planner®
P.O. Box 1702
Manchester, MO 63011

dianakoenig@hotmail.com

www.domesticplanner.com

ISBN: 1-58721-851-8

1stBooks – rev. 3/12/02

About the Book

   Domestic Planner® Systems was created to help people
cope in an increasingly complicated world. A recent survey tells
us something most of us already knew: We are spending more
time with our children than the previous generation, but we are
still working as much or more. When we try to cram additional
activities into an already impossible schedule, something has to
give. It usually ends up being the personal time we need and the
time we spend maintaining our homes. The information in this
book will introduce you to workable systems and principles that
will help you organize your life and manage your time
productively. You can reflect on each day with satisfaction
instead of guilt, and you can look forward to tomorrow knowing
you have a plan for almost anything that comes your way.

A Special Thank you

To my loving, patient, supportive, husband Paul,
my wonderful children,
Jennifer, Andrew, Brian, and Angela.
To my editor, teacher, and friend, Rick Perryman.

Table of Contents

Chapter 3: New Home Decorating 63

Chapter 4: Cleaning 81

Chapter 5: Planning Time Management 105

Chapter 6: Closets Drawers 141

Chapter 7: Basement Garage Outside 159

Chapter 8: Entertainment Parties 181

Chapter 9: Family Activities 211

Chapter 10: Children   233

Chapter 11: Organizing Your Family   257

Chapter 12: Holidays **279**

Chapter 13: Shopping **301**

Chapter 14: Maintaining Relationships **317**

Introduction

> Do you need more time?
>
> Are you submerged in clutter?
>
> Are you late for engagements?
>
> Is your life spinning out of control?

This book provides tried and true solutions that have appeared in my nationally published *Domestic Planner*® column. The information will help you organize your life and manage your time more effectively. I have successfully applied these principles in my home for many years and know they can make a difference in your life, too.

The Author

Home Organization

Clutter Free House

Q: Despite my best efforts, I usually come home to a cluttered house. What's the secret to keeping my house clutter free all the time?

A: You've had one of those tough days. You just want to leave the rat-race behind and get into some comfortable clothes or a hot tub. You open the front door and then it hits you: You walked out late this morning and left the home looking like the aftermath of a tornado. What a letdown! Wouldn't it be comforting to open your door each night to a calm, warm, inviting, and orderly refuge from the storm? This is the picture of a tidy, organized home. But if you want to consistently return to a clutter free house it requires designing a plan and implementing it diligently.

You have lots of ideas for keeping the house neater but you don't know where to start. Put action to your ideas! Start with a written plan. People who use written plans have a much greater success rate than those who rely on a mental one. Sketch out something that is practical and attainable. Title your plan **'Keys to a Clutter Free House.'** Before we make a list, let me introduce you to 'Ms. Clutter' and 'Ms. Tidy.'

Ms. Clutter wakes up in the morning and begins her day without direction. She wanders to the kitchen, pushing aside last night's dinner dishes so she can prepare breakfast. In frustration she looks for children's shoes and school bags because they were not put away the day before. Discouraged by the paper mess on

3

her counter she looks for a phone number so she can RSVP in regards to a dinner engagement just two days away. The phone rings and she scrambles to look for a piece of paper on which to write down a message. The pad of paper is not by the phone where she last left it. As she heads back to the bedroom to make the bed she decides to leave it unmade so she can change the sheets. She tries to recall when the linens were last changed but can not remember. Thoughts of a bubble bath and a time of leisurely preparation for the day swiftly pass as she enters the bathroom. She is confronted with bath towels piled on the floor, heaps of clothes scattered around, and a vanity pilled high with make-up, hair brushes, combs, toothbrushes, oozing toothpaste, wet washcloths, and an empty shampoo bottle. She has an early appointment and time is already running out. Now, she can't even wash her hair because she forgot to include shampoo on her shopping list. The empty bottle seems to mock her.

Ms. Tidy awakens each morning with a plan she immediately puts into action. First she makes her bed. Next, she takes care of her personal needs such as a shower, make-up, and fixing her hair. After checking on the needs of her family she enters the kitchen to prepare breakfast and lunches if applicable. When the dishes are clean and put away she freshens the bathroom with a quick cleanup. Her thorough bathroom cleanup will be saved for cleaning day. (Once a week a major cleaning takes place in Ms. Tidy's house. She spends this day vacuuming, dusting, changing linens, and scrubbing.) After leaving the bathroom, all wastebaskets in the house are emptied to prevent unpleasant odors. Finally, she quickly inspects each room, picking up items and putting them in their appropriate place. With a smile on her face, she leaves her well tended home for the day.

I function best like Ms. Tidy. The morning activities take me a little less than one hour. I move quickly but the amount of time to implement this routine will vary with individuals. Allow enough time to avoid frustration or unfinished tasks. The routine itself may also be different in each household. It is important to understand that Ms. Tidy maintains an organized house. You can not leave messes the night before and expect to wake up the next day and quickly tidy up the house. If you follow a regimen of continually keeping things picked up and put in their proper spot, leaving the house in order will be attainable.

Keys to a Clutter Free House:
- Make beds
- Clean-up kitchen, putting dishes and food items away
- Make sure each room is picked up
- Empty trash cans
- Do five minute bathroom clean-up
- Hang up clothes or put them in the laundry

Today's Refrigerator Bulletin:

"The trail that leads to a clutter free home requires picking up along the way!"

Household Piles

Q: My house is full of piles. I have piles of papers, laundry, dishes, and unidentified piles. How do I deal with this frustrating mess?

A: Deal with clutter piles before they merge into an insurmountable mountain. You will need to systematically eliminate the piles in your house. Identify and make a written list of the piles that continually accumulate in your home. You have created these piles or allowed other people to put them in your life. It is up to you to remove them and make a plan to keep them from recurring. I will discuss the most common household piles and outline a system for eliminating them.

Papers
Papers are the most common piles that create a clutter in your house. Deal immediately with every paper that you touch. Make a decision to file it or throw it away. Set up a filing system for papers you need to keep. Use colored folders designated for all major categories. Stacking papers on the counter, furniture, or floor should never be an option.

Unworn Clothes
Say good-bye to clothes that are dated, do not fit, you do not like, or you simply do not wear. Clothing your children have outgrown should be packed away for future siblings or shared

with a friend. It is difficult for me to give away clothes my children have worn because they hold special memories that I want to hold onto. One day I realized saving clothes from four children was creating many piles in my life. I spent several days going through all the clothing and saving a select few; the outfits they wore home from the hospital, an outfit from someone special, or a hand-made item. I looked in my photo albums to see if I had a photo memory of these clothes. I took a picture of the clothes that I didn't keep but wanted to remember. I then gave away all the unwanted articles.

Laundry

This is a pile you will have to discipline yourself to deal with daily. Doing laundry lends itself ideally to multi-tasking. You can put a load of clothes in the washer, another in the dryer and quickly move on to other tasks. Pre-sort by depositing soiled clothing directly into divided laundry baskets or hanging bags to eliminate separating each time you wash. You will need to train your family to put their dirty clothes in the correct receptacle. Fold clean laundry immediately and put it away. Do not throw it in a basket or on top of the dryer to deal with later: That is the beginning of an undesirable pile. When you have extra time, go ahead and do a load of laundry even if it is a small one. Select an economy cycle on your washer. By keeping dirty laundry at a minimum, you can maintain control of laundry piles during busier times in your schedule.

Movie Videos, Game Cartridges, CD's, Cassettes

Look at the area next to your entertainment center and see if every household member has put the tape or disk back into it's labeled container. If you have piles of tapes scattered around you will need to do three things. Devise a storage system that will allow access to each item without moving other items. Give away articles that have served their purpose, such as that weight loss video that didn't work. Items that are infrequently used should be stored in containers somewhere else in your house.

Leave room for growth in case you want to add to your tape and CD library.

Books and Magazines

Limit the number of books and magazines you own to the amount of storage space you have. Every book and magazine should have a home. Office stores and discount stores stock inexpensive magazine holders that fit on bookshelves. These magazine racks are available in many sizes and colors. Do not fill your shelves to capacity because you will always need room for growth. When you purchase a new book make sure you first have created a home for it on the shelf.

Little Pieces

Make sure little items such as paper clips, rubber bands, nails, and batteries have a home.

Separate them into small containers and place them in a drawer or box that is accessible to everyone.

Dishes

One dirty dish always has the potential of becoming twenty-five. Deal immediately with the one dish in your sink and you will never face a sink and counter full of dirty dishes.

Toys

If you do not want your house to look like a toy factory you will need to rotate toys so they are not all available at once. Select a few toys for your child to play with and switch the toys weekly or monthly. Your child will be excited to play with 'new' toys and you will not have piles of toy clutter. Train your children to put toys away.

Establish two principles:
- Deal with piles while they are small and easy to tackle.
- Purge your home of unwanted items on a regular basis.

Today's Refrigerator Bulletin:
"Eliminate an item or put it away!"

Organization Notebook

Q: I want to run my home efficiently but I have so much going on that I sometimes forget important appointments, phone calls, and errands. I could use a little help!

A: Managing a household is a full-time job. I like to use the title 'Domestic Engineer' for today's homemaker because it sounds important.   Maintaining a happy, stress-free home deserves an important title. To live up to the title, you will need a written plan that is practical and customized to fit the needs of your family. Research shows that people who write down their goals are more likely to achieve them. There are various daytime organizers and planners available, but are they practical tools to help manage a household? You may find that creating a custom home planner is a better option. You can build a basic plan to fit the needs and schedule of your family. Use the computer or hand write materials for your home planner. You will need to purchase a few inexpensive items such as a three-ring binder with a clear cover sleeve for a front insert, page dividers with tabs for labeling, and various colors of copy paper. You are now ready to create your own daily planner.

In the front cover sleeve insert a page on which you have written your last name and the title 'Home Plan.' Write the following categories on your tabs; Daily To Do List, Weekly To Do List, Errands, Phone Calls, Appointments to Schedule, House Projects & Repairs, Shopping List, Menus, and Children's Weekly Schedule. Next you will need to create a master sheet for each category. After creating the Master Sheets, select a paper color for each category and make several copies of the master sheet. Match the copies with the tabs you have labeled and put them in your binder. Store your master sheets in a plastic three-ring sleeve in the back of your notebook.

Creating your master sheets:

- Write at the top of the first sheet 'Daily To Do List.' Underneath your title write 'Day_____.' Number down the left side, one through eighteen, or whatever you have space for.

- Write at the top of the next sheet 'Weekly To Do List.' Underneath your title write 'Week of_____.' Number one through ten. Near the bottom of the page, write 'Relaxing Time' and number one through five. Don't forget to schedule time to relax and do something your really enjoy.

- Write at the top of another sheet 'Errands.' Underneath your title write 'Location' 'Things to Take' and 'Week of_____.' Number one through ten.

- Write at the top of a sheet 'Phone Calls.' Underneath your title write 'Person,' 'Reason,' 'Phone Number,' and 'Week of_____.' Number one through ten.

- Write at the top of a sheet 'Appointments to Schedule.' Underneath your title write 'Place,' 'Date,' 'Time,' and 'Phone.' Then number the sheet one through 10.

- Write at the top of another sheet 'House Projects & Repairs.' Underneath your title number one through ten.

- Write at the top of the next sheet 'Shopping List.' Underneath, write 'Groceries and Household Items.' You may also choose to use sub-titles such as 'produce,' 'meat,' 'toiletries,' etc. You may want to create a master list of items you commonly buy.

- Write at the top of the next sheet 'Menus.' Underneath, write 'Week of_____.' Next, list the days of the week, 'Sunday' through 'Saturday.'

- Make a sheet for each of your children. List the chores you would like them to do such as 'make your bed' or 'pick-up your room.' List the days of the week and ask each child to check off or put a sticker beside chores as they are completed. For children that cannot read, you can use a picture of the chore. At the end of the week, use the reward or consequence appropriate for your child's performance.

Your home plan is complete and ready for use. Some of your papers will be permanent fixtures in the notebook while others should be removed after they have served their purpose.

You need to keep your notebook in a location that is private but easily accessible for your daily use. This is your personal notebook and there may be information you will not want shared. Put your name, address, and phone number on the inside in case your notebook gets lost.

The final step is to faithfully use your new tool. Keep it with you, look at it often, and faithfully record the information.

Today's Refrigerator Bulletin:

"Organize your life with a customized daily planner!"

Fifteen Minute Plan

Q: I have read many books on organization. I have tried numerous suggestions and plans but my home is still a disorganized disaster.

A: Organization may not be your greatest area of strength but you can still improve your situation. Start with a mission statement. "From this day forth I will devote fifteen minutes a day to an organization task. I will schedule a specific time each day and allot additional time when it is available. Neither telephone, television, shopping, eating, nor any other device will separate me from my organization plan. I am determined to succeed."

Explore the benefits of functioning in an organized world. Be willing to invest the extra time and money now to create time-freedom in the future. A runner preparing for a race spends months training. He buys the best shoes. He fixes his eyes on the finish line and is willing to sacrifice now for future results. Along the way he will deal with setbacks, yet to succeed he must continue to train, set goals, and work towards achieving them. Apply these same principles to organizing your home. An organized home provides many benefits:

- More free time
- Increases your life span (it lowers your stress level)
- You accomplish more

- Boosts self-esteem
- Warm fuzzies (compliments from other people)
- Child training (contributes to your children's future success)
- Allows you to entertain with minimal effort
- You can enjoy an orderly home every day

Make a decision to rearrange your busy schedule and set aside time to become organized. It will take more time initially, but in the long run you will become much more productive. Your life is like a cluttered desk at the office. The desk is piled with heaps of papers that have an invisible stamp on them that reads, 'Urgent respond immediately.' Where do you go with all of the papers? Do you clear one corner and start a new stack? The only real solution is to invest time in creating a place for everything. Clear some filing cabinets. Label some folders. Only when you have done these important tasks can you eliminate the stacks, no matter how urgent they may be. The only alternative is to continue to move the same papers over and over again slipping further behind. Your time is much like the clutter of papers on the desk. Delete something temporarily from your schedule while you work your personal organization plan. You may even have to lose a little sleep. Once you achieve the desired organization level implement a maintenance system so you do not revisit your former lifestyle.

Organizing your life is a task that will demand your time and attention. Do not schedule it simultaneous to other major events or changes in your life, such as;

- A new pet
- A new baby
- Vacation time
- Beginning of a new job
- Extended house guests
- A major medical crisis

- A house renovation
- A family wedding

Once you confess the mission statement, focus on the benefits, and clear your schedule you are ready to conquer the mess. Make a list of the areas you want organized. Schedule time each day on an organization project. When an area is completed mark it off your list. Establish a maintenance plan to keep an area neat. If the pantry is your first battlefield, organize your pantry putting like items together. Stack or line up the canned goods putting the vegetables together, soups in the same area and so on. Maintain your system each time you put groceries away. When you are in a hurry do not be tempted to shove the canned goods in the pantry and ignore your system.

In addition to time, money is another required investment. You may need to buy containers or furniture to organize some areas in your home. You may choose to have a professional company install a closet organization system. Hire a home consultant to assist you. Reading books about organization is also a valuable tool to help you.

Observe the people around you that are organized. Use them as role models and ask them the secret to their success.

Today's Refrigerator Bulletin:

"Sacrifice fifteen minutes now to gain control of your future!"

Home Office

Q: I feel like I am an office manager for a major corporation. Along with our bills and important financial papers I need to keep track of manuals from household purchases, school notes, and information for sports. I also volunteer for several organizations. It is hard to keep all the papers, books, and forms separated.

A: You are the office manager for the most important corporation in the world; your home. Your corporation produces our future generation. Organization is just as important in your home as it is in a large corporation and for many of the same reasons. You have to manage receivables (paycheck), payables (bills), and purchasing (keeping your home furnished, the pantry supplied, and children clothed). To sustain this dynamic environment, you will also need to file and be able to access information about committees and organizations, canceled checks, financial statements, birth certificates, insurance policies, manuals, warranties, and even the magazine that holds the recipe with which you are anxious to impress your in-laws.

The ultimate solution is to establish a home ahead of time for booklets, manuals, receipts, and other papers. Keep everything separate and make sure the person that needs to access the materials knows where each is located. You would not want your notes on planning a 50's party to get lost in a stack of bills.

Designate a physical location in which to conduct your home business affairs. Ideally this would be an office or study. An alternative would be a designated work area in a corner of a larger room in your home. Make sure this is not a room in which you will entertain guests or allow young children to play. Whether you are scheduling a surprise party or paying a bill, keep basic supplies on hand so you do not have to scramble when a need arises. Minimum requirements include a workspace (table or desk), a phone, and a calendar. A computer, fax machine, and copier are added bonuses. Use a drawer or caddy for pens, pencils, calculator, ruler, paper clips, rubber bands, stapler, stamps, address labels, and tape.

Purchase a locked file cabinet for financial and other important documents. Label files by subject; birth certificates, vehicle information, mortgage and loan documents, tax receipts, social security papers, insurance, certificates, diplomas, paid bills, income tax information, budgets, and receipts. Using a portable file for unpaid bills allows you to pay bills in the doctor's waiting room or while waiting in the stands for soccer practice to end. Of course, paying bills is a more pleasant experience if you do it while watching a good movie. Keep the bills, stamps, return address stickers, envelopes, and a calculator in the portable file. You may also choose to keep a checkbook in the container if your system allows for it. Information that is extremely vital or sensitive in nature should be kept in a safe deposit box. Purge the files at the end of the year. Store items such as receipts and paid bill stubs in a box labeled with the applicable year. This will allow space for another year's worth of information in your file cabinets.

Buy a stack of colored pocket folders and designate a different color for each category in your files. Label the outside of the folder using a wide black marker. The combination of a clear, easy to read label and color-coding by subject will make finding information simple. These colored folders are inexpensive and readily available. They are easy to pull out and carry with you. If you are planning a school reunion you can keep everything pertaining to the event in one folder, taking it with you when you visit the potential event site or caterer.

The computer is a powerful tool to help you manage information in your home. Time and space constrain us from exploring all the possibilities of these wonderful machines. If you are fortunate enough to use a computer at home, remember two things: Keep hard copies of vital information, and always back-up (archive) important files.

New organization systems are a great but they are not always the answer. Be flexible to change the things that are not working efficiently for you. Your goal is to be organized and manage your time productively.

Today's Refrigerator Bulletin:

"Your home is a very important business to manage!"

New System

Q: I devour books and articles trying to find new ways to clean and organize my home. However, I still struggle with this area in my life.

A: Continue to read, do research, and apply new techniques. There are a few basic rules that are fundamental to maintaining an organized, clean home, but it is also a process of trial and error. Each household has different needs. Therefore you will need a customized plan and quite possibly a new perspective.

Fundamental rules that apply to every household:

- Clean your home weekly. This includes washing bed and bath linens, vacuuming, scrubbing floors, cleaning bathrooms, and dusting.

- Clean those hard-to-reach areas twice a year. This includes windows, baseboards, cleaning under furniture, and light fixtures.

- Keep closets, drawers, and cabinets partly empty to allow room for growth.

- Group like items and place them in separate compartments in closets, drawers, and cabinets by using plastic storage baskets.

- Make sure each item in your house has a home and that it returns to it's home. Items that are temporary visitors to your house such as library books, rented videos, and borrowed items need a temporary home.

- Devote one hour a week to an organization project in your home. This will help you maintain order.

You will need a customized plan because the amount of square footage and storage space is different in each home. The number of household members and schedules will also vary. Some households get extra help that may include a cleaning service.

I needed a plan to organize my sons' bedroom. Each of my daughters has her own bedroom but my sons share a room as well as a dresser, a nightstand, and a closet. Space is somewhat limited. Under the circumstances it would be very easy to cram their belongings together, but this doesn't set a very good example nor does it send a very positive message. Their organization skills not being the same as mine, I needed an organization system in their bedroom that was both effective and easy for them to maintain. Each son has two dresser drawers. For each son I placed a small basket in the middle of one of the drawers to separate clothing. I put white socks in the basket, dark socks on the right side, and underclothes on the left. Everything has a place and is divided to help keep items separated. The other drawer has folded shirts. I divided their night stand in half by using small plastic baskets so each of them has a space to call his own. In the closet I put several baskets on the floor. Each son has a large square laundry basket and two smaller baskets. The large basket is for jeans and sweat pants and the smaller baskets are for shorts and hats. It is easier than the old system in which their pants were on a high shelf: When they pulled down one pair, the remaining stack invariably followed. I group similar clothing together so they know where everything belongs.

Break out of your regular routine and try something new. Your traditional way of doing things may not always be the best. Move furniture around to add visual appeal and improve the traffic flow in a room. Add baskets and containers to closets and drawers. Lie or sit on the floor to get a different perspective of a room. With a different perspective you may notice something that needs to be cleaned that you have never thought about before. I pride myself on being a good housekeeper, yet I have been shocked at some of the cobwebs I have discovered while lying on my floors.

You may discover a new way to organize. During an in-home consultation I was helping a client organize the office of her home-based jewelry design company. We had spent the morning devising a plan to help her work more efficiently in her business. We organized supplies and equipment, prioritized current projects, etc. Although the client relied on my expertise for many tasks, she was very adamant about situating her desk. She wanted to situate the desk where she could to see her supplies and look out the window at the same time. After several unsuccessful arrangements, the client flopped into her chair, her back to the window. As we chatted, she stopped in mid-sentence as sudden inspiration swept over her. She realized the window had really been a source of distraction to her all along. She was sitting in the perfect position to work while allowing her a view of all the supplies and equipment in the room. She exclaimed, "I need to be like the conductor of a symphony. He faces his work, not his audience." Be open to change: It could drastically affect your life.

Today's Refrigerator Bulletin:
  "A new idea could prove to be rewarding!"

Too Much Stuff

Q: I never seem to keep up with cleaning and organizing my home. As I move from one area to the next, the first area is already a mess again. I feel as if I am on a merry-go-round. I am dizzy and I want off this ride.

A: Yours is a common problem. The answer may be as simple as this: You may just have 'too much stuff!' Over the years it is easy to accumulate a house full of treasures, especially if you move infrequently. Moving can rescue you because it works like a cleanser. We feel the urge to discard or donate items to a charity before the movers arrive or before we begin the packing process ourselves. Moving does not guarantee a 'house purging' but it helps. Obviously, it would be foolish to arbitrarily change houses simply to force this purging process. Instead, simply pretend you are moving every year and clear out some stuff. A good starter list of items eligible for purging should include clothing, knick-knacks, household items, and furniture.

If you have trouble parting with items you may be a 'house crammer.' If the following list describes you then be prepared for extra housework. Take the quiz to see if you fall into this category.

"House Crammer" quiz:

- "I can't part with this: It was from my favorite grade school teacher."

- "I know it hasn't fit in several years but it may fit after my next diet."

- "It does not match the room decor but if I redecorate in the future it will be perfect."

- "Isn't this cute? I must buy it! If I move a few items around I can put it on my dresser."

- "Just build more shelves in the basement and we can move everything downstairs."

- "These three walls in this room are filled but there is still a little space on this wall to squeeze something in."

Apply the following basic rules to help you conquer clutter and bust dust:

1. Decorate your home according to your schedule. If you are always short on time, keep your decorations simple. It takes time to clean and put items away. If you get more free time or hire extra help, then you can afford more decor.

2. You don't have to sacrifice the things that are important to you in order to decorate efficiently. Family photos are important to me and I like to display them in my home. I bought a floor photo frame that holds fifteen 8X10 photos. It fits neatly in a corner, is fast to dust, and does not create fifteen nail holes in my wall. I can enjoy family memories with little extra housework.

3. Purge closets, cabinets, and drawers every six months. Fill at least one box with items to be given away. Filling a storage area completely invites disaster. Keep each area 20% empty and it is more likely to stay neat.

4. Before you make a purchase ask the following question, "Do I really need this or do I just want it?" Just as too much food is harmful to an obese person, too much stuff can be devastating to a busy homemaker.

5. If your dresser is filled with knick-knacks they will share that space with just as many dust balls. Reserve the dresser top for a few special items. This will not only save you time but the items you choose will shine in their places of honor.

6. Do not fill every floor space with furniture, even if it satisfies a long desired wish. I had always wanted a baker's rack. I had money saved to make the purchase and had chosen a small space to erect the rack in my breakfast area. As I was scrubbing the kitchen floor one day I realized buying the rack would increase the amount of time it would take me to clean my kitchen. I decided I did not have time to spare at this point in my life. I will save the money for a future purchase.

Today's Refrigerator Bulletin:
    "Before an item finds a home in your house make sure you have space and time to clean it!"

Office Organization

Q: I have lost control in my office. I can't find important papers. I am missing deadlines on date-sensitive materials. I need help!

A: Organization is the key to productivity both in your home and office. Ask yourself the following questions. Am I comfortable when someone unexpectedly drops by my office? Can I schedule a last minute appointment at my office? Can I find the document I need at a moment's notice? If you can not answer 'yes' to each of these questions then you need a plan.

Lack of organization can negatively affect the way you conduct your business by undermining your self-confidence and producing unnecessary stress. Make a decision to do whatever it takes to organize your office. This means you must deal ruthlessly with your number one enemy: 'Paper Clutter!' It is easy to deal with one piece of paper but what about a stack of fifty? When we face a stack of fifty, paralysis sets in. You must overcome the paralysis, attack the stack, and develop a vision for the future.

To get organized and maintain order make a list of goals:

- Dedicate one hour a day specifically to tackling clutter.
- Find a permanent home for each item and piece of paper.

- Each piece of paper that you touch must be placed in it's home immediately. A home for a piece of paper is usually a file or the trash can. A home is not a pile on the floor, desk, or closet.
- Avoid the paper packrat syndrome. Do not keep unnecessary papers.
- Put like items together. This includes not only papers but also other items such as paper clips, envelopes, and rubber bands.
- Put items that you use frequently in the most accessible places.

Before you begin to organize your office make sure you have the space and supplies needed. You will need file folders, a file cabinet, stack trays, a wallboard or bulletin board, plastic baskets, and plastic containers with lids. Take time to visit your local office supply store. They usually stock everything you need to organize your office.

Unfortunately the computer age has not eliminated papers. In fact, in many instances it has created more. You will need to find a home for hard copies of your computer documents. Create additional space for these extra papers.

Once you have gathered your supplies you are ready to organize. Create a basic system before you pick up anything in your office. Make sure you have an empty file cabinet, empty shelves, a bulletin board, several stacked baskets on your desk, a large plastic container with a lid, and a box for trash. Think about the papers you will be filing and pre-label as many files as you can think of. It will be easier to act on each piece of paper if you have already created a home for the paper. Label some special files with the following names: Good Ideas, Five-Minute Break, Phone Numbers, Daily Agenda, and Weekly Agenda. The 'Good Ideas' file is the home for future ideas you want to implement. The 'Five-Minute Break' file is for things you enjoy doing. Periodically take time throughout the day to pull out the file and relax. Include in this file such items as a magazine to browse, a crossword puzzle, or a card to send to a special friend. The 'Phone Numbers' file is your back-up for important phone numbers in case you loose your daily planner or address book. Your 'Daily and Weekly Agenda' files are used to temporarily store papers that you need to act on in a day or a week.

Finally, begin picking up each item in your office. Make a quick decision as to where the item is going to live or make sure it immediately moves out of your office. If you struggle continually with indecision, consult an expert. This may be as simple as hiring a good temporary employee, asking your spouse or secretary to help you get organized, or hiring an organization consultant.

Today's Refrigerator Bulletin:
   "File it, please!"

House Maintenance

Q: **My home is clean and picked up part of the time, usually when I am preparing to entertain. The remainder of the time it is a mess. Is there any way to keep my home clean and organized all the time?**

A: Maintain whatever you organize, and clean regularly. Maintenance is the best way to avoid a huge mess in your house. Cleaning on a regular basis and putting items back where they belong is the simplest, yet most effective maintenance program I have found.

Clean routinely once a week and your house will look clean most the time. Then ask yourself the question, "Do I clean for myself or other people?" Our motivation will determine our degree of success. I clean for the pure satisfaction of living in a clean home. I do it for me. If I never had a visitor I would still keep my house clean. If you clean for others, you will only be motivated to clean when you are expecting visitors. This forces you to clean on demand (emergency cleaning is seldom convenient and usually not as effective). I know people who have done some very creative cleaning when they received only a few minutes notice that guests were arriving.

Here are some of their techniques:

1. If the dishwasher and the sink are both filled with dishes, carry the exposed dirty dishes to the bathtub but don't forget to pull the shower curtain in case your guests need to use the bathroom.
2. Fill cardboard boxes with household clutter and hide the boxes in the garage or the basement.
3. Of course, you can always shove any items littering the floors under beds or the couch.

I do not recommend these methods because they can be stressful. It is also requires a lot of extra work getting things back to their original location (like carrying all the dishes from the bathroom back to the kitchen). Establishing a cleaning maintenance program would be a lot easier. Your home would instantly be ready for guests and you could enjoy a clean home on a regular basis.

Keep your house picked up. This means putting everything back where it belongs when you are done using it. If you live with other people this can be a more difficult problem to tackle. It may require not only training yourself to put things away, but other household members will need to understand and practice this method as well. You may try a positive approach when someone leaves something out: "Honey, would you please put this back where it belongs?" If that approach does not work you might need to use negative reinforcement: "This item now belongs to me because you did not put it back where it belongs." Train yourself and your family to immediately return each item to its 'home' when it is no longer needed. When you need it the next time you will be able to find it quickly. It is so tempting to say, "I'll just put this on the counter for now and put it away later." Before we know it, we have accumulated an entire counter full of 'I'll put it away later' items. We have now increased the length of time it will take to put everything away because we have added a new element; sorting. We will have to sort through everything before we put it away. Other family members may not share the same philosophy as you. They may feel that leaving something out is more convenient because the item is in plain view where they can access it quickly. I would rather take a positive approach with them but I am prepared to use, "It's mine now." Maintenance means putting away each item as soon as you are finished using it.

Today's Refrigerator Bulletin:
    "House maintenance equals house in order!"

Temporary Problems

Q: Could you please help me with this problem? Things that do not belong to me create messes in my house. People come over and leave their umbrella, books, gloves, serving dishes, toys, etc. We do a lot of entertaining which causes us to accumulate items that do not belong to us. All of these items end up in the way. They are usually on my counter as a reminder to give or return to someone. I buy gifts ahead of time. What do I do with gifts before I give them?

A: This is a problem that plagues us all. Often, people visit our homes and leave their possessions. Items constantly rotate in and out of our houses. You collect umbrellas, silverware, jackets, gloves, books, watches, and numerous other items. You need a system to ensure the safe return of these items to their appropriate owner. A workable system will also prevent these items from cluttering your counters.

Another related problem is remembering to return borrowed items. If a friend loans us a good book and we want to remember to return it to her as soon as possible we need an appropriate place for the book. We face the question, "Where do we put the book until we can return it?" A similar predicament occurs with gifts we buy for people.   Bargain shopping is a fantastic way to buy gifts ahead of time but then we need a place to store the gifts. Leaving the gifts out on the counters is not an option. Cramming them in a closet could make it difficult to access them or remember they are there. We continually face the problem of temporary items in our house. A solution to this dilemma is to create 'rotating shelves!'

Rotating Shelves: Create two empty shelves in your house in a location you look at often.

'Rotating shelves' are essential to keeping you organized. Choose two empty shelves in your house. If you do not have empty shelves you may need to create them by moving items around. Mine are in my hall closet. This is a good location because I open this closet daily. Use these shelves to rotate items you keep for a short period of time. These items include library books, gifts, borrowed items, and items left at your house. Besides owning many books that they keep in their room, my children also borrow books from the library. This causes a problem. The library books and personal books are mixed together. I cannot monitor the due date so this results in library fines. The rotating shelves solved this problem. I put the library books on the rotating shelf and the children's books are in their rooms. I can stay abreast of the due date because I see the books daily on my rotating shelf. This is also a perfect shelf on which to keep gifts that you will be giving within a week. I have a shelf in my basement on which to store gifts I buy long before giving them. Wrapped and unwrapped gifts are on the rotating shelves. The greeting card, wrapping paper, and gift are kept together until the gift is ready for wrapping. I can see what is on the shelf often because I have chosen a good location. Get in the habit of checking the rotating shelves when a friend stops by or when you go to visit friends so that the items can be returned to their owners.

There are times when these shelves are empty and other times when they are very full. Add a third shelf if your first two are constantly full. Your need to rotate items may be greater than mine.

Today's Refrigerator Bulletin:
   "Empty a couple shelves in a frequently used closet to house the items that come and go."

Organization Recipe

Q: I have tried many times to better organize my life. I have read books on organization and talked with people that are organized. I have concluded that I am a failure in the area of organization.

A: Adopt the motto, "If at first you don't succeed try, try again." You are not a failure and you have probably been successful in areas of organization that you do not recognize. Do not try to become organized overnight. It takes time to make major changes in your life. Organize your life step by step just as though you were following a recipe to bake a cake. I have written an organization recipe that will bring order to your office, home, room, closet, cabinet, and drawer.

Carefully follow the recipe. Each ingredient is important and must be measured exactly to produce organization in your life.

Basic ingredients to organize your life:

2 cups (create a home for each item)
Separate like items together
1 cup (find a home for each new item that enters your home)
4 tablespoons (get rid of items you do not use)
3 cups (return each item to it's home when you are done using the item)
¾ cup (keep empty space in drawers, closets, and cabinets)
2 pinches (laughter)
Fold in 1 ½ cups (relaxation)

Sift out the paper clutter in your house
Stir away lumps of discouragement until smooth

Measure 2 cups of creating a home for each item in your house. Make sure each family member knows the home. Separate like items together using baskets and plastic containers. Add a cup of finding a home for items that you buy or things that are given to you. Immediately find a home for each item that enters your home or office. This will reduce clutter. Make sure you purge unneeded items on a regular basis. Return an item to it's home when you are done. This will avoid the accumulation clutter monster.

Add ¾ cup of empty space. Make sure drawers, closets, and cabinets never exceed 80% so you have room for growth. It is important to blend in laughter and relaxation because without time out, organization may fail because of stress and discouragement. Sift out paper clutter daily to avoid accumulation. Immediately tackle mail, school papers, and work documents. File or discard each item. Stir vigorously until the batter is smooth and ready to be baked.

Baked at 350 degrees for one hour to obtain perfection! Remove immediately. "Do not put off until tomorrow what can be done today."

Baking tips:

- It is important to add each ingredient on a consistent basis
- Take plenty of time to measure each ingredient
- Make a fresh batch each day

Today's Refrigerator Bulletin:
"Make sure you include each ingredient for an organized life!"

Phone Calls

Q: It is difficult to respond to the all of the phone calls I receive. I forget to return some of my calls or I misplace the number, which usually turns up a day or two later.

A: It is important to respond to the people who contact you. If a person has taken time out of her schedule to call you then you should respond to her in a timely manner. Your failure to respond may cause her to draw inaccurate conclusions. She may think you are rude, insensitive, and disorganized. You cannot use the excuse you are too busy. We live in a busy society. Everyone is busy! Most people fill every minute of their time with an activity. You should respond to every phone call even if only briefly. Zero response is not an option. A better alternative would be to call the person and simply explain you only have a window of time but you wanted to respond to their call.

Make a plan to respond to each phone call:

- In your home and office keep a notepad and pen by each phone. If there are other people who are responsible to answer your phone let them know the information you will need.

- Create a phone log with basic information. Across the top of the page write 'name,' 'time of call,' 'phone number,' and 'reason for the call.'

- When you check your answering machine, call notes, or voice mail keep a note pad handy to write down messages.

- Once you receive a message that requires a response make a written plan to return the call. Return the call immediately or make sure you have a written reminder. Our memory is not the most reliable source.

- Caller ID is an excellent way to retrieve numbers and names that are recorded incorrectly.

- Until you have all the facts, do not prejudge a phone call and decide not to respond.

- When you return a phone call and need to leave a message on an answering machine or with someone else, respond a second time if you do not hear back. Answering machines accidentally get erased and people forget to convey messages.

- Some returned calls are unpleasant but necessary. Compose yourself before making the call by engaging in an activity that relaxes you such as reading a book, enjoying a cup of coffee, deep breathing, or a physical exercise.

- Some calls take time but not concentration. You basically need to be a good listener but not an intense listener. Use a portable phone and multi-task. You can fold laundry, pick-up clutter, pay bills, or do anything else that does not produce a lot of background noise.

- Some calls require silence or privacy. Prepare your household before making the call. Let everyone know you can not be disturbed. If you have young children allow them to watch a favorite video. You can put a toddler in a playpen with a toy he has not played with in a while.

- Make sure you have a comfortable phone to use.

Today's Refrigerator Bulletin:
    "Protect your reputation by responding quickly to phone calls!"

Money
Management

Coupons

Q: I have a box filled with coupons. I grab a handful on the way to the store only to discover they have expired. How do I organize my coupons so they are useful?

A: Manufacturers have come up with a scheme to give away money, so we might as well take advantage. You can save a significant amount of money using coupons, but the serious coupon clipper must have a system. The specific system you use will depend on the amount of coupons you save, but all successful 'Coupon Queens' need three elements: good coupon sources, easy access to the coupons, and a good working knowledge of the cost of goods and services.

Coupon Sources:

- Coupon books are worth the investment. They range in price from $5-$30 depending on the size. Using a few of the coupons usually pays for the purchase of the book.

- Most yellow pages offer coupons in the back of the book.

- Newspapers run coupon offers and usually include coupon inserts in the weekend edition.

- Stores offer coupons at their courtesy counter or on racks in the front of the store.

- Scout for coupons in magazines.

- Many items have coupons for same-day or future purchases printed right on the packaging.

- Ask friends, neighbors, and relatives to give you newspapers and magazines they are discarding. You may even trade extras on a regular basis with other coupon clippers.

- Look for promotional coupon packets in the mail.

Accessing Coupons: Unless you have a workable system to store and access coupons, even the most avid shopper will quickly get discouraged. Many coupons have been clipped and left to expire without ever seeing the light of day. To avoid this, buy a plastic filing box with a handle and files, labeled with the following categories;

- Entertainment (movies, video rental, museums, plays, sporting events)
- Restaurants (fine dining, fast foods, and pizza delivery)
- Services (dry cleaners, carpet and upholstery cleaning, oil change)
- Repairs (Home repairs include electrical, plumbing, furnace, and appliances. Car repairs include brakes, muffler, and tune-up.)
- Groceries
- Travel (lodging and transportation)
- Purchases (clothing and household)
- Free (Always use coupons that give you something free. Check this file often.)

- Rebate (Keep separate envelopes for each rebate offer. Keep receipt, bar code, and form in this envelope until you mail the rebate to the company.)
- One month (Place coupons that will expire in a month in this file. Look at this file often.)

Some categories, such as groceries, should be divided into sub-categories. Within the file, create subjects such as dairy, cereal, meats, breads, bakery, frozen, etc. Separate restaurants into groups: fine dining, fast foods, and pizza.

Using Coupons: Your storage system for coupons should be portable because many of the coupons are used away from your home. Keep them in a file box with a handle that can be easily carried about and placed in your car.

Look through your coupons often so you will know what is available. When possible, base your choice of restaurants, services, places to visit, and food items on the coupons. Those that offer 'buy one, get one free' provide great savings and are readily available.

Some grocery stores advertise double or triple coupon days. Take advantage of these offers whenever you can. Such offers often include only those coupons worth fifty cents or less. And remember, many brand name items are more expensive, even after using coupons, than equivalent generic products at regular price. Use common sense!

This same principle applies to services, but since we use services less often, we must be educated consumers. Just because a business offers a 20% discount doesn't mean they have the best deal in town. We had an emergency plumbing problem in our home. I looked for a coupon that offered a discount for a service call. I called several companies from which I had coupons only to find out their prices with the coupon offers were generally higher than those I normally paid without a coupon. It is important to know the prices of items and services when you use coupons.

Today's Refrigerator Bulletin:
   "Save money with a system that organizes your coupons!"

Household Budget

Q: I never have enough money to manage my household the way I want. Providing for the wants and needs of my children is important to me. I realize I need to tell them 'no' sometimes, but I really believe I have enough income to tell them 'yes.' I just can't seem to make it last.

A: Select one of the following responses to the question, "How well do you stay within your budget?"

- What budget???
- You budget for household items and usually manage to stay within the budget.
- You've tried several different budgets that seem to work for short periods of time, but none has ever worked for you in the long run.

There are no cookie-cutter budget solutions. Establishing a successful budget requires effort on your part to find out what works for your household. Money, like time, slips quickly through our fingers. To prevent this from occurring you need to not only plan a workable budget, but also faithfully adhere to it.

The advantages of a budget are:

- You know exactly how money is spent.
- You can funnel money in the direction you choose.

- You have the opportunity to save money for a future purchase, event, or vacation.
- Functioning within a budget teaches your children fiscal discipline and responsibility that they can carry into their own future households and families.
- Your careful planning and discipline can prevent future financial disaster.

Begin by making two lists: income and expenses. List income from all sources as accurately as possible. This is relatively easy for those on a fixed income, or those who receive a regular, predictable salary. Other households depend on commissions, seasonal work, or income that is often affected by unpredictable circumstances such as weather. If you fall into this last category, budgeting is more difficult but not impossible. You will simply need to look back six months or a year to determine a workable budget.

After determining your income, list all your expenses. Start by listing each fixed expense including house payment or rent, car payment, and insurance. Estimate variable expenses such as food, gifts, and car repairs. Although every list of expenses will be different, many of the categories will be common to almost every household.

A typical list would include; housing, car payments, loans, utilities, phone, insurance (car, life, homeowners, health), taxes, medical, food, gasoline, gifts, entertainment, children's allowances, car repairs, house repairs, business expenses, clothing, charities, education, sports activities (dance, baseball, soccer, etc.), postage, disposable items (cleaning supplies, toiletries, paper products), retirement and/or savings, and miscellaneous.

Add all your income in one column and your expenses in another column. Are the two figures the same? If the income number is higher than the number listed under expenses, your system will succeed. However, if the opposite is true, you are headed for financial failure. You will need to cut expenses and/or increase your income. Cutting expenses may mean changing your spending habits. Review your needs and see where you can cut back. Food is one area you may be able to make an adjustment. Bargain shop all the grocery stores in your area, taking advantage of the sale items each store offers. Plan your meals according to what is on sale instead of what you feel like eating. Cut back on the money designated for entertainment. There are many fun things that are free or inexpensive. Making a date to eat peanut butter and jelly sandwiches in the park is less expensive and can be just as fun as eating at a five-star restaurant. You accomplish the most important thing: Spending quality time with someone you love.

When you finally balance the income and expenses columns, determine which system you will use to manage the household budget going forward.

1. Envelope system. Weekly or monthly, divide your available money into marked envelopes for food, gifts, etc. Use the money in the food envelope, for example, to buy groceries. Pace your spending so that you do not end up with an empty envelope and an empty cupboard before the end of the week or month.

2. Open two checking accounts. Designate one checking account to pay bills such as house, utilities, car payment, etc. The other account would be for flexible expenses such as food, clothes, entertainment, etc.

3. Use one checking account. Save each receipt and tally the amount spent on a master sheet listing each expense. Put receipts in the envelopes that you have clearly marked with date and contents. Not only will this give

you a clear and accurate picture of what you are spending, it will give you a jump-start on taxes each year.

There are budget workbooks and computer programs that will assist you in managing your household budget.

Today's Refrigerator Bulletin:
"Time spent planning a budget is worth the investment!"

Receipts

Q: **I can never find receipts when I need them. Sometimes I need to return items to the store or I need to locate a receipt for tax purposes. How do I organize receipts?**

A: Receipts often end up in stacks with our other paper clutter. In most cases, we will never need to see them again. However, we occasionally need to locate a receipt. Sometimes we need to return or exchange clothing or household items. We may also need to return a spoiled food item. If we have our receipt, the transaction goes more quickly and we receive a cash refund instead of a store voucher.

Develop a system to organize your receipts. After you make a purchase, put the receipt in your purse in a small envelope. This is a temporary location until you arrive home. In your house you should have a home waiting for the receipt as well. One good system for organizing receipts involves using large envelopes or file folders. Every year, start with several empty envelopes or folders, each labeled with the current year and a category. For starters, you might use the following categories; groceries, small and large appliances, clothing, tax deductions, car repairs, gifts, medical expenses, home improvements, and miscellaneous. As new categories are needed, add another envelope or folder. At the end of the year, file the receipts with that year's taxes.

If you find that you have several receipts from a single vendor in a folder, you may want to group those receipts within a category, or even create a new folder for them. For instance, if you frequently visit a local discount store you can paper clip those receipts together in the folder or envelope. Other groups you may choose to paper clip together could be photo developing and restaurant receipts. You could set up separate envelopes or folders for each of these, but unless you have a large amount of receipts in a specific sub-category it would be better to simply paper clip like receipts together to avoid having so many envelopes or folders. Write the name of the subdivided category on a slip of paper and slide it under each paper clip. This will help your household budget by making you aware of what you are spending in the different areas of your life.

Another method to organize your receipts is to use a shoe box or plastic container about shoebox size. Write the year on the box. Label index cards with the appropriate categories and insert them in the box to use as separators. At the end of the year use a stapler or paper clips to keep 'like' receipts together.

Here are some tips to help supplement or enhance your system. For keeping track of receipts from small appliance purchases, save the original box. Keep the receipt with the box until the warranty has expired. You may consider using a separate plastic container or shoebox to keep you miscellaneous receipts. You will accumulate more miscellaneous receipts so you will need more storage space. When you buy a gift for someone, use a pencil to write his name by the item on the receipt. I save all my receipts when I Christmas shop. I put them in an envelope and write 'Christmas' on the outside. I write the person's name on the receipt and paperclip the price tag to the receipt. It is easy to locate everything if I need to make an exchange.

You never know when you will need information about purchases. If you use a system to organize your receipts it will help you to access this information. You may need to know what car expenses you have incurred. You may want to know how much you have spent on photo development. The amount of money you spend monthly on groceries could be valuable information. You will be able to locate all the receipts quickly with this system. This information will help as you plan your household budget.

Today's Refrigerator Bulletin:
"Keep those little slips of paper and file them efficiently!"

New Home
Decorating

Furniture Organization

Q: We recently decided to redecorate our Family Room with new furniture. Decorating is not my gift so I am at a loss about what style to choose and how to arrange the room.

A: There are many things to consider when you decorate a room and buy furniture. You must consider the size of the room, color scheme, how the room will serve the needs of your family, and how long you intend to keep the new decor. It is important to research the cost before you plunge into decorating or buying furniture.

- Visit many furniture stores to see what is available. It will give you an opportunity to explore your personal taste. You can also ask about discounts. Many times you can negotiate price, especially on a large purchase.

- Choose furniture according to the needs of your family. Light colored or slick upholstery does not hold up as well under heavy use or spills and stains. A medium colored, textured fabric would be a better choice. Dark colors show lint and can be a nuisance to care for.

- Buy furniture to fit the size of your room. Use large, bulky, furniture only in a large, open area. Keep plenty of space and clear paths in your room. It is not time efficient to walk around furniture traveling from one room to another.

- Before you purchase your furniture decide on room focus. Furniture is commonly arranged around an entertainment center, fireplace, or in a grouping conducive to conversation.

- Ottomans are comfortable for relaxing and reading. They do not work well for constant entertaining. They take up space and provide a temporary resting place for people's dirty shoes. Consider alternatives, such as wingback chairs with hidden footrests. They serve nicely for entertaining as well as those relaxing moments.

- Provide tables and coasters for drinks but do not encourage eating and drinking on your furniture. Spills are inevitable. Do not serve dairy drinks or beverages containing red dye. Both of these have the potential to damage your furniture.

- Take into consideration your flooring, curtains, and wall decor before you buy new furniture. You need to match what you have or be prepare to buy matching flooring and window treatments that fit the new scheme or style.

- Buy furniture to accommodate your entertainment patterns. If you frequently host meetings or parties buy padded folding chairs for extra seating. Do not fill your room with furniture: Reserve floor space for the temporary chairs.

- Arrange your room for multiple purposes. A semi-formal room with wingback recliners and sofas arranged for conversation or reading can quickly be transformed by turning the chairs toward a television set concealed in a hutch. Large floor pillows can provide additional seating and create a more casual atmosphere.

- Choose less expensive furniture if you re-decorate often. It doesn't need to stand the test of time. If you plan to keep it forever, buy the best you can afford.

- When your room is complete establish some household rules. No shoes or dirty clothes on the furniture.

Today's Refrigerator Bulletin:
"Decorate your room according to your taste and needs!"

Windows

Q: Every time we move, I face the difficult task of choosing window treatments. Can you suggest some easy and inexpensive options? How can I keep window treatments looking fresh and clean?

A: Windows are a very important part of your home. If you want to fully understand how important windows are, imagine your home without any. They are worth the effort it requires to decorate and care for them because they provide your home with natural light from the outside. They help introduce the elements of nature into your home, enlarging your world. At night, windows become warm, inviting beacons of hospitality.

With all of its benefits, direct sunlight will fade fabric on furniture and carpets, damage photos, and make your air conditioner work harder in the summer. The windows also allow others to visually intrude into your sanctuary. The obvious solution to both of these problems is window treatments, which can accent the theme of your room and provide a decorative bridge between the wall covering and the flooring. It is important to consider all of the major elements of the room (the flooring, furniture and wall covering) when selecting window treatments.

Window treatments can range from very expensive to simple and inexpensive. Installing custom lined drapery or hiring an interior decorator will minimize your effort but will cost you more. If you are on a tight budget, tackle the project yourself. You can glean many ideas from magazines and books. You can also visit display homes to accumulate a wealth of good ideas. If you purchase window treatments, get washable, no-iron fabric to avoid expensive trips to the cleaners and time spent ironing.

Besides using standard curtain rods, which come in a variety of styles and sizes, you can pull material through decorative brackets or drape or wrap fabric over decorative headers. Perhaps a valance or cornice could be used to enhance the look of the window. A valance can be made of fabric gathered into ruffles or pleats and hung on its own rod in front of the longer drapes. The valance can also be stuffed with newspaper or tissue to create a balloon valance. A cornice is a valance consisting of a board (wood or masonite), covered with upholstered fabric and attached to the top of a window frame. You do not have to limit yourself to fabric only. After installing a valance, add color and pizzazz by stenciling around the rest of the window.

You do not have to follow a traditional look: Experiment and invent new, unique ideas. In one bay window, I gathered each side of the curtains and tied them with ribbon. I planned to attach the gathered curtain to a hook on each side of the window, but I liked the appearance of the curtain hanging in the middle so much, I repeated it with the pairs on the remaining windows. In small areas such, as a sunny breakfast nook, you can gain space by inserting the curtains on a spring rod inside the window instead of on a rod projecting from the frame.

Once you have decorated the windows, you need to maintain their beauty through routine care and cleaning. Dirty windows distract from the window treatment. Thoroughly clean your windows at least twice a year or hire a company to do it for you. There are numerous products on the market you can use to clean your windows. You can also use a vinegar and water solution.

Wipe the windows with paper towels or newspapers. Avoid using rags because they leave lint on the glass. To locate smudges, examine the glass from both directions.

Clean your window treatments twice a year. Lined draperies will need to be removed and vacuumed or wiped down with a cloth. For stains or a more thorough cleaning, they will need to be sent to the cleaners. Encourage family members to keep their hand off the window treatments. Sticky fingers and oil from hands will increase the frequency of cleaning. If you keep the window treatments simple you will spend less time cleaning them.

> **Today's Refrigerator Bulletin:**
>   "Picture Perfect"

Moving

Q: Moving is difficult because there are so many things to remember to do. I feel disorganized and frustrated. How do I organize a move?

A: We have moved several times, and each move presented its own unique challenges. One fact was consistent through each one, moving is always easier if I plan and organize. The only reliable way to plan and implement a move is to keep a written list. There are different things to do when moving to a new city or state. You must familiarize yourself with stores, cleaners, service stations, and schools. Besides knowing the location of places you need to change your driver's license, apply for a grocery check cashing card, and open a bank account. It is important to be flexible and be ready to implement plan B when plan A fails.

We rented a house for nine months while we were building a home. We moved into the rental property from another state. I made the move while seven months pregnant and with two small children. I had my written list but I had to adapt to some unexpected circumstances. The moving van arrived one day later than expected. The men that were scheduled to unload the truck never arrived. My husband and extended family helped unload instead of doing the other tasks I had scheduled for them.

Due to the many setbacks and fatigue from pregnancy I sat on the steps crying as I directed each container to the proper room. I learned a significant lesson from this experience. Planning is good but flexibility is an absolute must.

The system I use to prepare for a move:

- Moves are complicated enough. I use the simplest system in existence. I label the top of a piece of paper with the words 'To do List.' When I think of something that I need to do, it is written on this list. When I accomplish a project on the list I draw a line through the task.

- Moving is an excellent time to get rid of items. I schedule a garage sale before the move and give the remaining items to a charitable organization.

- We list our home with a Realtor and begin looking for a new home.

- I minimize purchases at the grocery store prior to the move. I try to use the food we have or give it to a neighbor.

- I clean out every closet and drawer in my house. I am in the mood for a new beginning so it is amazing the number of items I get rid of.

- I may begin purchasing new decor items, drapes, and linens once we have the new house selected. I have to pack a few extra boxes for the move but once we arrive I can begin to decorate my new home immediately. This small niche of order among the chaos somehow helps me to maintain my sanity.

- The day of the move I pack the car with bed linens, towels, toiletry items, and a couple of changes of clothes. This will avoid the problem of hunting for these items the first night in our new home.

- Once the house we are leaving is empty I clean the bathrooms and vacuum.

- When we are in our new home I clean everything before I begin unpacking. I make sure the furniture is placed in the middle of the room. If we have possession of our home a few days before the big move I spend the time cleaning and hanging window treatments.

I follow the same procedure whether a moving company moves us or we move ourselves. I make sure the closets and drawers are organized so 'like' things are packed together. I file papers in their appropriate place. I clearly label each box. If I am responsible for the move I start packing early. The more time I organize as I pack the easier and faster it will be unpacking in the new home.

Today's Refrigerator Bulletin:
"Organize your packing for a smooth transition from old home to new!"

Room Decorating

Q: I have saved money to redecorate my family room. Hiring an interior decorator is not in my budget but I want it done well and in a timely manner. Could you give me some pointers?

A: Decorating or redecorating is enjoyable but is also a big job if you are the 'interior decorator.' You can find success and satisfaction when you take time to organize everything you do. In the past few years I have redecorated several rooms in my house, one of which was my family room. I like to have things neat and in order so I am particularly intolerant of stepping over ladders, paint cans, tools, or looking at empty walls for more than a couple days. If you share my aversion you must carefully plan the renovations. You will not want to move furniture, remove pictures from the walls, begin painting or wall papering until you have written a schedule and purchased construction materials, furniture (if applicable) and decor.

Procedure for decorating a room:

1. Visit display homes, look in magazines, observe other people's homes and look in furniture stores to get ideas. If you are not an interior decorator by profession you will need to train yourself by research and observation. Avoid being trendy but still try to be current with styles

and colors. After making a decision on the theme of the room, decide on the style and colors.

2. If you are buying new furniture, your next step is to visit several furniture stores so you can find what you like and get an idea of prices. Allow additional lead-time in case furniture needs to be ordered.

3. Choose wall covering and/or paint to coordinate with the furniture. Be a frugal shopper, allowing plenty of time to purchase these items on sale.

4. Go on a shopping marathon to find wall covering, pillows, wall decorations, lamps, and other decor. Compare prices, look for sales and then make your purchase.

5. After you purchase everything, schedule the appropriate amount of time to take the old down in order to prepare for the new. The first two days, empty the room and paint and/or wallpaper. Hold the furniture at the warehouse and schedule delivery when the walls are completed.

6. Decide what to do with old furniture and decor when it is removed from the room. You may choose to use it in another room in your house, sell it at a garage sale or give it to a charity.

7. Prearrange to have the carpets cleaned after the walls are painted or papered and before the furniture is delivered.

8. After cleaning the carpets or floors, clean the windows and put in all decorations not directly dependent on furniture placement.

9. Decide where everything else will go before the furniture arrives. Have the furniture delivered, hang remaining wall decor and arrange all other accent pieces.

When I decorated my family room this process took two months from start to finish. We changed everything in the room; furniture, walls, window treatments, wall decorations and other room decor. The only thing we did not change was the carpet. The actual time it took once the old things were removed was one week. We finished the painting on a weekend but could not coordinate carpet cleaners and furniture delivery until the end of the week.

When my sons decided they had out-grown the train and sailboat decor in their room I allowed them to help choose their new room decorations. We looked through catalogs and decided on a theme. I purchased items and brought things home for their approval because browsing around town for a good deal was not their idea of fun. Allowing them to take part in the decision making and decorating teaches them organization principles and makes them feel important. I spent time with my children while accomplishing a household task.

Occasionally something happens when I am playing interior decorator that causes me to panic. One such thing happened when my husband and I redecorated our bedroom. I had completed my plan, made all my choices and purchased the materials. My mother-in-law had sewn and quilted an heirloom quilt around which I planned the rest of the room. My husband had agreed to let me change our room from a masculine look to pink and lace Victorian. I removed everything from the room except the blue carpet and we proceeded to paint the walls mauve. Upon completion of one wall I burst into tears because mauve walls and blue carpet were not a good match. I was sure I had made a decorating mistake. In compassion my husband said, "Honey, it's OK I'll just re-paint with any color you would like.

His encouraging words were all I needed to continue painting the walls mauve and proceed with my plan. After the stenciling was done, the lace curtains were hung, decor was arranged and the antique white furniture delivered I had a room fit for a Queen!

Today's Refrigerator Bulletin:
"Appoint yourself Interior Decorator of your home!"

Cleaning

Meticulously Clean

Q: Each week I make plans to thoroughly clean my home. At the end of the week I realize something else has snatched my time. I tried my mother's system of deep cleaning my home a week in the spring and a week in the fall but my career and children's activities prevented this plan from ever happening. Help!!

A: It is difficult to find time to clean your home if you manage a career and provide a taxi service for children's activities. Even more difficult is finding the time to 'deep clean' periodically, but deep cleaning is an absolute must. If you hire a cleaning service you will still need to deep clean once or twice a year. One method I have used successfully is to include a few extra cleaning projects in my regular weekly cleaning day. Although this works for me, I have had to come up with some creative contingencies when my schedule gets really busy. If you really want a clean home, it takes more than just a desire; it requires a decision! This decision will need legs, and that's where a plan comes in. Finally, your plan will need some backbone. That's where the two 'D's' become important; discipline and determination.

Your routine cleaning schedule should include the following: wash the bed and bath linens, dust, vacuum, scrub the floor, clean the bathroom, and pick-up clutter. But what is included in your extra cleaning chores? I have listed mine so you can make a comparison. In each room I do the following, starting from the top and moving down:

- Dust ceilings with an extended lamb's wool duster.
- Clean light fixtures and ceiling fans.
- Wash walls, paying special attention to the light switches.
- Move furniture, dust or vacuum the entire piece including the back.
- Clean windows.
- Clean vents.
- Wash baseboards and doors with a wood cleaner.
- Wash drapery, bedspreads, and mattress pads.
- Clean and reorganize closets, cabinets, and drawers.
- Remove cushions from furniture and dust.
- Clean fireplace if applicable.
- Periodically remove several items from each room. Give items away or store them in a box of keepsakes in your storage area. Most of us have too much stuff.

This is a long list to complete on your own 'precious' time. Enlist the help of your family. This will accomplish two things: You will get the help you desperately need and it will teach your children responsibility. Schedule a time with each of your children to clean his or her room. Prepare for them a list of what you plan to accomplish in their rooms. Use this time to discourage the 'pack-rat' syndrome. Children, like adults, have special treasures that quickly fill all free space and begin to pile up as clutter. Teach them how to say good-bye to items. Give or throw these items away. As an alternative, take a photo of some items and begin a keepsake album or store items in a keepsake box. As a reward for their help, take them out for an ice cream treat or special lunch. Here are a few other ideas for accomplishing your organization goals:

Enlist the help of your husband for your bedroom, the garage, and the basement. Show your appreciation by fixing his favorite dinner or save money from the household budget to take him to dinner and a movie.

Hire a teenage helper or your own children to tackle the remaining rooms in your home. This labor is inexpensive compared to a professional cleaning service.

Schedule a time to clean each room in your house. Write it down on your calendar and diligently adhere to the schedule.

When you complete cleaning each room buy one new decor item for the room. It will give the room a new, fresh look and reward you for your hard work. Plan to make this purchase from your household budget. For example: I save $5.00 from my grocery money to buy a new towel for the kitchen or a scented candle for the bathroom.

Finally, spray air fresher in the room and admire your masterpiece.

Today's Refrigerator Bulletin:
  "Your home will sparkle with discipline and determination!"

Spotless Bathroom

Q: Our bathroom is the first room to become cluttered and dirty. I want a clean bathroom with minimal effort.

A: Imagine walking into your bathroom and smelling the scent of a spring day. As you enter the room you observe beautiful hanging linens, sparkling fixtures, and fresh flowers. This dream can be a reality if you are willing to clean and maintain. Your bathroom is usually the smallest room in your home yet it is one of the rooms most frequently used. It can go from clean to disaster area in a few brief moments. Limited space usually equals a cluttered castle. Continual use of a space means it requires extra attention. Since we often refer to the bathroom as the 'throne room,' we should treat it royally.

You can minimize the workload and enjoy cleanliness by systematically cleaning. The number of people that use the facility will determine the amount of time and effort you clean. A heavily used bathroom should be thoroughly cleaned each week. This should include:

- Vacuum and scrub the floors.
- Scrub the bathtub, shower, toilet, and sink.
- Clean the mirrors with a good glass cleaner.
- Hang clean linens.

The following tasks should be done each month. I like to incorporate them into my weekly cleaning, doing a few each week:

- Dust the light fixtures.
- Polish the faucets.
- Clean the woodwork; baseboards, cabinets, and doors.
- In tiled areas, whiten the grout with a cleaner or bleach solution.
- Buy a cleaner to eliminate soap scum build-up.
- Dust wall décor and silk floral arrangements.
- Wipe the wall close to the light switches.
- Clean the windows if applicable.
- Wash off the shower curtain if applicable.
- Straighten items in the drawers, cabinets and closets.

In addition, daily maintenance is a must for bathrooms. Below is a list of daily tasks:

- Wipe the mirror, sink, and toilet with the appropriate cleaning solutions.
- Empty the trashcans. In a small space a full or partially full trash can make a room look cluttered. I empty mine a couple times a day.
- Hang or place fresh hand towels on the vanity. I do this several times a day for germ control.
- Wipe the shower door with a dry rag after each use. This will avoid the accumulation of soap residue and mildew.
- Remove any hair that falls into the sink. Eventually the hair will clog your drain. Avoid brushing your hair over the sink.
- Each person should rinse the sink thoroughly after he brushes his teeth.
- Keep a rag and cleaner under the sink to be used for a quick clean up.
- We have improved our bathroom facilities over the past century. Think how far we have progressed from the

original backyard 'out houses.' Some homes have bathrooms that are as large as bedrooms. Many of these larger bathrooms have a separate shower and tub instead of the traditional combination. You can also find bathrooms with two sinks, a large vanity, and a walk-in-closet. You will need to schedule more time to clean these larger areas.

Decorate in a manner that will make your time in the bathroom a pleasant experience. Decorating possibilities for bathrooms are endless, but limit the quantity of your decorations or you will increase your cleaning time. It will be easier to clean the sink vanity, tub, ledges, and the back of the toilet if decorations are kept to a minimum. Do not decorate the bathroom with heirlooms, photos, or special keepsakes. Moisture and mold are inevitable in this room and can be destructive to these items. Reduce bathroom mildew by providing plenty of light and good air circulation, and use a disinfectant cleaner.

Keep cabinets and drawers partially empty and use small plastic containers to separate groups of items. To keep from passing germs, store toothbrushes so they do not touch each other, especially during flu season. Rinse your toothbrush thoroughly with hot water after each use. Fold bath towels, washcloths, and hand towels into separate stacks. Do not over-stack and make sure linens are easily accessible.

Your bathroom can smell fresh if you include scented candles, potpourri, scented room spray, or fresh flowers. A pleasant scent makes for a pleasant bathroom. A burning candle destroys odors. I burn scented candles when I entertain in the evening. The candle also provides a beacon to the bathroom if the light is off.

Today's Refrigerator Bulletin:
   "Maintain a clean, fragrant throne room!"

The Art of Cleaning

Q: I really do not like to clean my house. There are a million other things I would rather do yet I seem eternally condemned to this daily task. Help!

A: Many people share this aversion to house cleaning. Fortunately, cleaning does not have to be a daily task. Establish a weekly house-cleaning routine so you will not feel as though you are cleaning every day. You will need to control the clutter on a daily basis, but do not confuse cleaning with managing clutter. Picking up clutter does not qualify as cleaning.

The first step in making cleaning less drudgery is to change your attitude. Granted, society does not rank house cleaning very high on the pay or prestige scale. Yet, cleaning is a vital part of properly caring for virtually every material item in your life, so clean your house with pride. Cleaning your house is as important as any other career. You have worked hard to establish your home and the contents therein, which represent a vast amount of your time and money. It is an honor to be entrusted with their care.

If you choose to hire someone else to clean your house make your choice carefully. You are entrusting a stranger with your life's precious treasures. You do not want to fill the position with someone who will sweep through your house quickly just to get the job done. You might have to pay more for someone who is good, but you can also expect more.

If you delegate specific cleaning tasks to your family, make sure you educate them on how to properly do the job. This is not merely a meaningless, repetitive task you are asking them to perform. Explain to them the importance of their work and your purpose in creating an atmosphere of excellence.

Clean with passion, as if you were painting a masterpiece. You will be presenting all of your meticulously crafted and beautifully framed household masterpieces to family, friends, and most importantly, yourself.

A clean house will give you a sense of security, freedom, and peace.   You will not experience embarrassment when unexpected visitors show up at your door. You can go to sleep at night with a feeling of peace and contentment because your house is in order.

Each item in your house is woven together to create your home, a place of refuge and relaxation from the outside world. Do not let anyone fool you into thinking cleaning is not a very respectable job. You are not just dusting a dresser or scrubbing a floor. You are the caretaker of your castle.

Today's Refrigerator Bulletin:
   "Clean your household masterpieces with pride!"

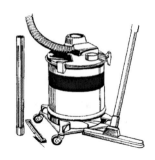

Cleaning Schedule

Q: I am about to hire someone to clean my house. How do I train this person to clean my house efficiently and thoroughly?

A: Whether you are training yourself, one of your children, or an outsider, start with a cleaning plan. First choose a day of the week that works best in your schedule to clean your home. After you have chosen a day make a list of the things you want cleaned. You will want a basic plan that includes things like dusting, vacuuming, and scrubbing the floors. You will also want a custom plan that includes specific tasks unique to your home. You may want to concentrate on cleaning areas that bother you the most. Some people are bothered by dust while others can tolerate a little dust accumulation but want their bathroom to sparkle like the morning sun.

Basic Plan Example:

Bathrooms: Clean toilet, vanity, shower/tub, mirror, vacuum, scrub floor, wash linens, hang clean linens, and empty trashcan.

Bedrooms: Strip beds, wash bedding, remake bed, dust furniture & knickknacks, vacuum floor, and empty trashcan.

Kitchen: Wipe and disinfect counters, refrigerator, stove, range, dishwasher, microwave (inside and out), vacuum, scrub the floor (including inside pantry), dust chairs, and empty the trashcan.

Living Room, Dining Room, and Hallway: Dust furniture & knickknacks, and vacuum floor.

Laundry Room: Wipe off the washer, the dryer, shelves, counter, vacuum, and scrub floor.

If you have an office, sunroom, library or other rooms include them in your basic cleaning plan. In addition to your basic plan you will need to add 'extra' cleaning areas.

Extra's Example:

- Wipe off baseboards
- Clean inside of vents
- Take cushions off couches and vacuum
- Clean all light fixtures
- Clean cabinets
- Clean behind and under washer & dryer
- Clean behind and under refrigerator
- Clean light switches and the surrounding wall to remove fingerprints
- Vacuum with a hose around baseboards
- Vacuum closet floors
- Dust window ledges
- Clean windows
- Dust blinds
- Sweep garage floor
- Sweep porch and front walk
- Move furniture in each room to vacuum
- Wipe walls in soiled areas
- Clean bedspreads

- Clean drapery and curtains

Once you have compiled your list make a five-week schedule. Week one will be the first week of the month. It will include your basic plan plus any additional areas you want cleaned that particular week. I assign these extra areas by dividing monthly tasks into four groups and doing one group each week in addition to the basic plan. Apply the same procedure for weeks two, three, and four. Week five will also start with the basic plan but the extra items on week five should only include areas that need to be cleaned quarterly. Quarterly tasks may include something like cleaning the baseboards. You may want some items such as washing the windows to be on a six-month or yearly cycle. In this case you will need to either add an additional cleaning day once or twice a year or extend the time you clean with the five-week plan.

Put your five-week plan in a three-ring binder. Store your binder with your cleaning supplies or your vacuum cleaner. Your written five-week plan will help you to accomplish your cleaning goals or give clear instructions about your expectations to anyone you have hired.

Today's Refrigerator Bulletin:
"A successful five-week cleaning plan."

Cleaning and Clutter Control

Q: I need tips on how to keep my house clean and clutter-free.

A: It is an awesome responsibility to maintain a clean, clutter-free house. Listed below are ideas on how to create a simpler home environment so you can minimize the time you spend as clutter policewoman and cleaning lady.

- Consistently clean your home. Make sure you schedule a weekly cleaning time.

- A big house takes more time to clean. Allow for extra cleaning time.

- Small houses with limited storage quickly become cluttered. You will need to purge items often.

- Use under-cabinet mounting for appliances to keep counters clutter-free.

- Minimize the number of items you display on dressers and tables. Dusting will be a breeze.

- Use shower curtains with liners instead of shower doors. It is easier to clean a shower curtain and replace a liner than to spend time scrubbing mildew and water deposits on shower doors.

- Control the mildew in your bathrooms by having plenty of light, good air circulation, and use a disinfectant cleaner.

- Place baskets on the counter tops in your bathroom for items you need at hand such as make-up and lotion. When you clean the counter it is faster to pick-up a basket than the loose items. It is also easier to clear the vanity top of items not currently in use.

- Identify the home chores you do not enjoy and come up with creative alternatives. For example, if you do not like to clean the fireplace consider using your fireplace differently. Place large candles inside the fireplace and burn them. This allows you to create a pleasant atmosphere without the mess. Add scented candles and your room will have a sweet aroma.

- Use large rugs and runners at the entrances to your home. The rugs can grab most of the dirt from shoes before they enter the rest of the house. I recommend you and your immediate family take shoes off at the door.

- Rough sidewalks knock off dirt from the bottom of your visitor's shoes.

- Whenever possible leave enough space between furniture to vacuum.

- Make sure you can easily get behind and under furniture to clean.

- Do not put furniture in front of windows. You want easy access to the window for cleaning panes, dusting sills, and window treatments.

- To save folding time, wash bed linen and immediately return the sheets to the bed.

- Shades are easier to clean than mini-blinds. Keep mini blinds clean by dusting often. If they become extremely dirty wash them in the bathtub or on the driveway with a hose and a scrub brush.

- Black furniture and glass are harder to maintain. Black furniture shows dust very quickly and glass tops show fingerprints. Medium colored wood furniture requires low maintenance.

- Wipe the microwave each time you use it. It takes only ten seconds to wipe a clean microwave but it could take 30 minutes to remove baked-on food particles.

- Install light fixtures that are not intricate and hard to clean.

- Minimize the use of silk arrangements. Cleaning flowers and leaves is time consuming.

- Light carpets show dirt; dark carpets show lint. Choose a medium colored carpet.

- Furniture on rollers such as beds and refrigerators can be moved easily for cleaning.

Your new systems will save you time when cleaning and picking up clutter. Use the extra time to treat yourself to a fun activity.

Today's Refrigerator Bulletin:
 "Simplify your home whenever possible!"

Cleaning Supplies and Equipment

Q: Cleaning the house is a never-ending hassle. I am not even sure what supplies and equipment are best to use or where I should keep them.

A: It is important to have the proper cleaning supplies kept in an accessible storage location. You certainly do not want to spend time searching for window cleaner. Likewise, if your vacuum cleaner is buried underneath closet clutter you will not relish the idea of pulling it out to clean.

Store your vacuum cleaner in a clutter-free closet. Make sure the cord self-winds or can be easily wrapped. A central vacuum system is great for multi-level homes. If you do not have a central vacuum system, purchase separate vacuum cleaners for the upstairs and downstairs levels. Carrying a heavy vacuum cleaner up and down steps can be tiring and dangerous. It may even cause you to vacuum less frequently, compromising your standards of cleanliness in the home. You want a vacuum cleaner with adequate suction and a head that covers a large enough area so you can swiftly clean a room. Good suction is more important than fancy features. Keep plenty of vacuum bags on hand. An over-flowing bag will drastically reduce the cleaning ability of the machine. Keep the attachments in a basket or bag on a hook near the vacuum cleaner. Attach a large hook on the wall in your closet for the hose. Make sure you can get to everything conveniently.

Crumbs accumulate quickly in kitchens and dining areas. You will not be anxious to pull out the vacuum cleaner after each meal. Instead, keep a small hand vacuum cleaner or broom in the pantry, garage, or mudroom. At times, I simply use a rag and wipe up the area on my hands and knees. It is fast and good exercise. You will decrease the amount of vacuuming required if you wear house shoes or slippers in the house instead of street shoes. My household follows this shoe removal rule and I only vacuum once a week.

Buy basic cleaning supplies and limit the amount of extra supplies you purchase. Minimize the use of waxes and polishes on furniture and floors. They cause build up and yellowing. Completely read the labels of every cleaner. Do not mix bleach with other cleaners unless you have checked to see it is safe. Remember bleach whitens everything including carpets and furniture. I have ruined clothing items because I have put them on a counter where they absorbed unseen droplets of bleach.

Often, you can substitute safer and less expensive food-based items for harsh chemical cleaners. A vinegar and water solution is effective for cleaning mirrors and glass. Lemon juice whitens and removes many stains from counter tops.

A couple of basic options exist for storing cleaning supplies. Option 1: Keep supplies in one location such as a shelf in your laundry room. Store cleaning supplies and several rags in a caddy. Limit the amount of cleaning bottles and sprays to the space in the caddy. If space is limited, store a back-up supply in another location. You will want a caddy that can easily be carried around the house. Keep a bucket by your caddy to use for larger clean ups. Cleaning supplies should be in a location inaccessible to young children. Option 2: Keep cleaning supplies in the actual locations around the house where intense cleaning is most needed. Usually, this will include each bathroom and underneath the kitchen sink.

Post a pad of paper in your kitchen to list the supplies you need to buy. Write each item on the list as soon as you notice the supply is low. Don't wait until the container is empty. When cleaning day comes, you will greatly appreciate a good inventory control system. Unplanned trips to the store consume enormous amounts of time.

Today's Refrigerator Bulletin:
"Minimize the time you clean with accessible equipment and the right supplies!"

Planning
Time Management

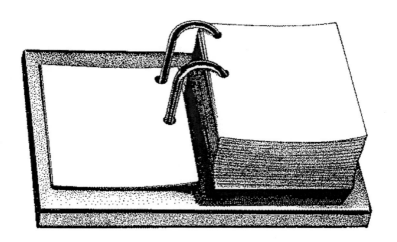

Organization Commitment

Q: I want to organize my life and spend my time productively but I am so busy. When I start an organization project I am constantly interrupted.

A: Several enemies prevent us from becoming organized. You must face each of these enemies individually and overcome them one at a time. Only then can you proceed successfully with your plan to be organized.

Enemy number one is a busy schedule. If you are drowning take a close look at your current schedule. Are you over-committed? Write down everything you do in a week. Examine your list and circle the activities that you must do. See if you can delete any activities that are not circled. If you are going to devote time to organizing your life you will need to free up some time from your present schedule. Many people volunteer for almost every committee, class party, field trip, and leadership position that they are asked to take. These people are personal organization disasters. You will increase your level of productivity and be a greater help to others in the long run if you first get your own house in order.

Another common enemy is simply a lack of knowledge. You may want to be organized but lack the knowledge to make a good plan, much less put one into action. Read materials on organization. Consult organization experts. Talk with people who posses these skills. Educate yourself in this area if you want to be successful.

Procrastination is another enemy that you face. You may want to be organized but you continually put off tackling this important task by choosing to do other things. There is no magic formula for overcoming procrastination. You need to repeat these words to yourself; "Just do it!"

The people with whom you live may not share your vision for becoming organized. They may undo everything you try to establish. In this case, you might stir up controversy by doing something as simple as organizing the junk drawer. Perhaps you have spent a couple hours arranging containers and grouping like items together. You place the scissors in one container, paper clips in another, rubber bands together, etc. Your son uses the scissors and neglects to return them to their established home. When you remind him, he becomes angry because it has always been okay for him to leave the scissors on the counter. You not only face the prospect of training yourself to be organized, but you must also train your family. Take time to train them using a reward or punishment system. Do not allow them to become an enemy to your plan.

Our own attitude and decisions will determine our success. If you make organization a priority and ignore all excuses you will succeed in this area of your life. Both my husband and I have careers that demand hours of our time. In the late fall we made a decision to paint the outside of our house completely before Christmas even though my husband arrived home from work each night after dark. His solution was to paint by floodlight at midnight. A few months later we trenched and mulched our yard in the darkened spring night. We did not allow our schedule or the midnight hour to prevent us from accomplishing our goal.

Choose your own time line for becoming better organized. Choose to devote a minimum of one hour each week to work on an organization project. For a more aggressive plan spend one hour a day organizing. Make it your goal to become better organized.

I accomplish my dreams and goals by first obtaining the **knowledge** I need. Second, I **discipline** myself to work towards reaching my destination. Third, I am **determined** to succeed. Finally I package everything with **passion** for reaching my goals. I can do this with something as simple as organizing a closet. Observe the people that are successful in the things they do. They have passion!

Today's Refrigerator Bulletin:
"Remove your enemies and apply knowledge, discipline, determination, and passion to becoming organized."

Time Off

Q: I need more time to myself. I work many hours and rarely have time to relax and socialize with friends. I am stressed and tired. Help?

A: First, think about what relaxes you? Imagine lying on an ocean beach with a gentle breeze, listening to the waves lapping against the shore. Consider the possibility of receiving a $500 gift certificate for a shopping spree. What about a day with nothing to do? Make a mental list of what sounds relaxing to you and then put your list into action by scheduling "Time Off!" Schedule your relaxing time the same way you schedule work, appointments, errands, household chores, and carpool. The busier you get the greater will be your need to relax.

Each person will have a different list. What relaxes one individual may add stress to someone else. Camping, boating, and climbing a mountain could either relax or add stress to your life. Let's look at a couple examples: Suppose your career involves constant reading. Reading a good book in the park may not be a good way for you to relax. Suppose you are a golf instructor. Golf is a form of relaxation for many people but you may need a different activity. Relax with purpose. Participating in activities that are relaxing will rejuvenate you. You will work at a higher level of efficiency and actually accomplish more if you take time to relax.

Suggestions for relaxing:

- 15 minute delight! Try each day to schedule one or more 15-minute periods in which to relax. Use this time to eat a favorite food, browse through a catalog, manicure your nails, do a facial, look at photo albums, read a book, play a game with one of your children, write down an idea, write a friend, call a friend to chit chat, or sit and do absolutely nothing.

- Shopping is very pleasurable. This does not always mean spending money. You may find it relaxing to browse and dream about plans to decorate a room in your home. You may spend months or years planning a room before the finished product becomes a reality. The planning can be fun and relaxing.

- Talking with family and friends is fun. Schedule one or more of these times each day. This should be a time for enjoyable conversation, not conflict resolution.

- Consider taking up a physical sport like tennis, golf, bowling, dancing, or roller-skating. Schedule this time regularly with a friend or your spouse. Try to improve your game but basically play for fun.

- Schedule a regular time to meet a friend at a restaurant for lunch or dinner. Chatting over food is relaxing, especially if you did not spend time preparing the meal.

- Arrange a game night with family or friends. Serve snacks as you play board games, word games, or card games.

- If you enjoy creative activities, schedule a time to sew, quilt, paint, or work on another craft that is of interest. Be adventurous and try something new.

- If you enjoy taking photos, do something special with them. Put them in a photo-safe album, write down important events and decorate with stickers and colored paper. Photo scrapbooking can be very relaxing both in the creation and later as you open your masterpiece to reminisce. It is like looking at a storybook about the memorable events of your life.

Today's Refrigerator Bulletin:
"Work towards relaxing!"

Time Savers

Q: Time is something I never have enough of. The needs of my family and my household chores pull constantly at my time. I need a quick easy solution.

A: Time is something you may always scramble for. Although there is not an easy solution you can find better ways to manage your time efficiently. Identify those areas where you think you are wasting a lot of time. Focus on doing them more efficiently.

Does laundry demand a large portion of your time? Consider enlisting the help of your family and make some changes in the way you do the laundry.

- Buy divided baskets or divided laundry bags to separate clothes as they are put into the laundry. Your family can sort the clothes, although you may have to educate them where to put darks, whites, and bright colors.
- Most people separate their clothes by colors, but you can also separate in other ways. Wash all the towels that belong in the master bath in the same load. You can also wash clothes that drip dry together versus clothing that you place in the dryer.
- Buy a different colored laundry basket for each family member. Put their clean folded clothes in the basket. It

can be their responsibility to put the clothes away and return the basket to the laundry room.

- Pin socks together before washing so you do not have to match them or end up with a single sock.
- If you leave a load of clothes in the dryer too long you can throw a damp washcloth in the dryer and dry for another 5-10 minutes to remove wrinkles from clothes.
- Fold bath and kitchen towels so they are ready to hang without refolding them.
- Hang pants and clothes on padded hangers so you do not have to spend time pressing out wrinkles.
- Clothespin gloves and mittens so you will always have the pair.
- Stack towels and linens with the folded edge pointing out so you can quickly grab just one.

The kitchen is another time consumer.

- Make sure you store items close to the location you use them. Pans close to the stove, silverware, glasses, and dishes close to the dishwasher.
- Arrange items in your cabinet and drawers so the items you use most frequently are in the front. Put items you seldom use up high and in dead space.
- Put an old tablecloth under the highchair or under young children while they eat.
- Keep daily medicines in the kitchen cabinet so they are close and convenient.
- Apply adhesive tape or felt squares to the bottom of your kitchen chairs to avoid leaving marks on the floor as chairs are scooted around.
- Use a pump soap dispenser and a spray hand lotion. These are items you use several times a day and you will want fast access.
- Keep your kitchen smelling clean and fresh. Grind a small lemon slice in your garbage disposal and simmer

an orange in water on the stove. This will relax you and reduce your anxiety about time.

Other household time saver tips.

- Keep a shoe box or plastic container for purchase receipts. Whenever you make a purchase put the receipt in the box so you will be able to find quickly if you need to make a return.
- Let the answering machine take your calls when you are pressed for time or in the middle of a project.
- Keep a pencil and pad of paper close at hand so you can list items to buy and things you need to do. You will not have to think about it and your mind can focus on accomplishing your current project.
- Color-code your keys so you can identify them quickly.
- List home chores that require only a five-minute window of time. If you pop into the house between car pool runs, do one of the chores on the list: fold a load of laundry, change bed linen, unload the dishwasher.
- Keep color-coded file folders handy for current activities in your life. Include children's activities or committees on which you serve.
- Keep a list of frequently called numbers by each phone.
- Buy a stair basket with a handle in which to place items that need to move to another floor. You will avoid cluttered stairs and constant trips up and down.
- Near the end of each month check your calendar for the upcoming month's birthdays and anniversaries. Fill out the cards and stamp and address the envelopes. Write the required mailing date on a note and stick it to the envelope.

Today's Refrigerator Bulletin:
    "Save a minute here and there each day and suddenly you'll have an entire hour to spare!"

Implementation

Q: I need more time each day. As more things slip through the cracks, I feel like my life is out of control. My house is a mess, and I forget important engagements. Is there hope for me?

A: Time is a precious commodity of which we never have enough. You can not buy more time, so you need to become more efficient with the time you have. This will require organization in your life. Becoming organized requires discipline and perseverance. Keep in mind that the extra time it takes now to organize your life will yield much more time later for the things you enjoy doing.

The road to organization and controlling your time is like any other journey. You must first plan an itinerary, then prepare for the trip. Since you have an entire lifetime to get organized, let's compare it to a leisure trip in which you have no real drop-dead arrival time. First, you must decide where you are going. This would compare to setting realistic goals for organizing your life. Next, you must make preparations that will cost you time, pain, and possibly money. Go at your own pace and do not feel threatened by those that zoom by you quickly. Like an extended tour, your itinerary will change as you discover interesting side-trips or are forced to take detours around dangerous obstacles. The only thing you can be sure of in this journey is that nothing

119

will ever stay the same. Things rarely go as we plan so we must prepare for the unexpected. Use setbacks and detours as opportunities to evaluate and look at the map. You may discover an alternate route or a short cut. Short cuts are okay if you know where they lead. Make sure you take time during your journey to relax and sightsee.

The trip you are going to take is the road to an organized life. You must pace yourself as you travel this road and remember it is not a race but a destination you hope to reach. You will eventually get there, whether you choose to crawl, walk, or run. Do not be discouraged by roadblocks. Faithfully practice the motto, "If at first you don't succeed try, try again."

Time can be our enemy: When we fail to plan, it is quickly snatched away from us. Make a written plan to become better organized. Start by making a list of how you spend your time. See if you can delete some activities from your schedule by numbering them in degrees of importance. Then schedule a specific time weekly to work on an organization project in your home. You determine how much time you have, but plan to spend a minimum of an hour a week. Protect this time and do not allow anything else to fill it unless you have a true emergency, not to be confused with an 'urgency.'

Make a list of the things in your life you want organized. Post your list and one by one begin tackling the projects during the time slot you have designated for such tasks. When we allow everything to be urgent and eat up our time, we focus on these 'emergency' projects or activities and never tackle the extras.

Let's use house clutter as an example. If you live in disarray you will have difficulty finding things you need: Items become temporarily or permanently lost. You spend an enormous amount of time looking for things. This time is not productive and eats into other things you need to be doing. You can choose to change this situation or continue to 'function' in the chaos.

If you decide to eliminate the house clutter then this is the road you have chosen to travel. How do you navigate this road? Map out your plan. Make a plan to spend two hours a week picking up clutter and creating a home for each item you touch. Follow your plan faithfully except for emergencies. Continue this process until everything has a home. This could take weeks or months depending on the state of your house.

You will face detours on your road to a clutter-free house. In order to create a home for items you may need to clean out some closets, drawers, and cabinets. You will need to box up items to be given away or discarded. This will temporarily create a bigger mess in your house. Just as you should not focus on the fog but the road you need to think about organizing space in the closet, not the mess you have created in the process.

When you feel you have a conquered the clutter in your home beware lest you return to your old ways. Always return each item to it's home when you are not using it. Strongly encourage every household member to do likewise. Choose another road to travel that will help you manage your time more efficiently. Perhaps the next leg of your journey should explore the answer to the question, "How do I maintain a clean house?"

Today's Refrigerator Bulletin:
   "Follow the road to organizing your life more efficiently!"

Goals

Q: I am so ambitious about planning things, but I never seem to accomplish much. I feel disorganized because I manage my time inefficiently.

A:Set goals! Successful people set goals and work towards accomplishing their goals. There are different types of goals: Long-term goals, short-term goals, personal goals, work goals, constant goals, and temporary goals.

Write a list of your goals. Research shows that people who write down their goals are more likely to reach them. If you have difficulty getting organized each day, take a few minutes the night before to write a list of what you hope to accomplish the next day. Visualize in your mind the start of the next day. This will help you to be ready. Check things off as you complete them. This will give you a sense of accomplishment and keep you motivated.

Everyone has different goals. It is important when setting goals to measure them against your standards and expectations, not the expectations of others. Some people need a working surface totally clear of clutter before they can prepare dinner or pay bills. Others function just fine with piles of papers pushed to the side. I work best with the surface totally clear. Therefore my goal would be different from those who function fine with clutter around them.

Your goals need to be realistic. Think about what bothers you the most. Are you always late to appointments, meetings, or other engagements? Are you frustrated because you constantly misplace items? Does your kitchen floor always seem to be dirty? If these things bother you, set realistic goals based on problem areas in your life.

Work patiently and slowly towards reaching your organizational goals. You were not born organized so you must train yourself in this area. Crash diets and cramming for exams are not very successful. Master one goal before moving on to the next.

Setting goals may involve changes in your life. Start with the one thing you want to change the most. Write down what needs to be changed, how your life would be improved by the change, a plan to implement the change, and a list of actions to make the change. Focus on an area that frustrates you the most. Once you have successfully made a change in one area, repeat the process with another area of your life.

- **What area of your life needs to be changed?** Example: I am frequently late for appointments.

- **How would your life be improved by making this change?** Example: I would no longer suffer the embarrassment of showing up late for appointments.

- **What plan would you use to implement the change?** Example: Set the timer to ring at the appropriate time to leave.

- **What action will be taken to implement the change?** Example: I have a dental appointment on Monday morning at 8:30. It takes fifteen minutes to drive to the dentist's office. I need to set the timer to ring at 8:05 so that I can prepare to leave the house ten minutes early. It is important to allow extra time in case something unexpected occurs.

When something becomes routine or you become proficient in an area, you no longer need to write it down. I have a goal to maintain a clean, clutter-free home. One way I reach my goal is to routinely clean each week. This is the day I thoroughly clean. I do not schedule lunch, golf, errands, or shopping on this particular day. With rare exceptions, I consistently accomplish this goal. I no longer have to write this down.

Goals help you accomplish what you want to do. To fulfill goals you must specify dates and times. You will want to make two separate lists: constant goals and temporary goals. A constant goal might be to drive carpool every Mon., Wed., and Fri. from 8:00 A.M.-8:45 A.M. This goal rarely changes. Remembering to wrap a shower gift for a friend would be a temporary goal. Upon completion, the need for the goal goes away.

Today's Refrigerator Bulletin:
"Make changes according to your needs!"

Productive Day

Q: Each day I feel as though I should be accomplishing more. How do I increase my daily productivity?

A: Ask yourself the following questions: What determines a productive day? Who sets the standards for a productive day? Unless someone is paying you wages, do not measure productivity by someone else's standards. We are often disappointed by our productivity because we subconsciously base our standards on the expectations of others. This makes us demand far more of ourselves than others would normally ask. Decide what it would take for you to experience a productive day, regardless of those around you. If you were recovering in the hospital a productive day might simply include eating a meal and taking a short walk down the hallway. For a mom with young children a productive day might boil down to feeding, clothing, napping, and providing a safe environment for them.

You may work full-time outside the home or you may spend your days as a full-time mom volunteering on school committees and driving children from one event to another. Whatever the career, you soon discover clutter collects, dust gathers, laundry baskets explode, and dinner is served from a bag or a box. If you can not tackle everything, then do something you know you can finish so you will feel productive. Spend a few minutes dusting the family room before retiring for the night. File a few papers that have accumulated on the kitchen counter or fold a load of laundry that is piled in a basket. Doing only one of these chores will not take long but can give you a sense of accomplishment.

View productivity differently. Do not always measure your success by how many items you scratch off your 'to do list.' If you took ten minutes to send an encouraging note to a friend, imagine how productive that act of kindness would be.

How do we increase productivity? The most successful way is with written goals and several back-up plans. The combination of these two tools will increase your productivity. Let's say everything you plan goes haywire. This can cause stress and discouragement. No matter how much you organize and plan you life there are circumstances beyond your control. We usually call these bad days, but sometimes an entire week refuses to go according to plan. You can still salvage the day if you train yourself to plan and allow for flexibility. I recently was reminded of the importance of these two objectives. I was scheduled to pick up my son from a Cross Country race at 1:30 p.m. I arrived on time but the return bus he was riding did not. It was over an hour late. Neither my son nor I had anticipated this long delay. I read through my 'do to list' that I keep with me at all times. Although my afternoon was fully planned I spent the time productively by choosing a back-up plan: I wrote this column.

Another important way to increase your productivity is to build relaxation into your schedule. You should always plan some activities that you enjoy. This is fuel for your emotional tank. If your tank is empty you will not run, and you will have nothing to give to the other important people in your life.

Today's Refrigerator Bulletin:
    "Find something productive in each day!"

Waiting

Q: I rush to appointments or activities and then end up waiting. What a waste of time!

A: Everyone experiences the familiar routine of 'rush-wait.' It is discouraging to rush for an appointment and, upon your arrival, be informed you will have a half-hour wait. A similar experience occurs when you hurry to be first in the carpool line, only to wait an additional twenty minutes for school dismissal. We spend time waiting at the doctor, dentist, sports activities, carpool, and meetings. While we are waiting we suddenly realize all the things we could be accomplishing during this wasted time. Be prepared and this wasted time can become productive time. There are numerous things you can do in these five to forty-five minute waiting periods. Some activities would only work in the surroundings of your car while others could be done in a waiting room. Determine what you will do based on the amount of time you think you will have to wait.

Use a tote bag to rotate your planned activities. One day it may be filled with a mending project and a book. The next day you may choose to rotate those items out and put something else in your tote. Always keep a pencil and notebook in your tote. Carry this tote bag with you to the car each time you leave.

Suggestions to fill your time while you wait at appointments or activities:

- Read a book or a magazine.

- Plan a party. Decide on a theme, decorations, food, and games.
- Plan a weekly menu. Remember to pack some cookbooks so you can try a new recipe.
- Make a grocery list.
- Plan a vacation. Think of a place you have never visited. What activities would your family enjoy? Take maps, brochures, and vacation guides with you.
- Write lists of goals. Short-range goals could include errands or household chores for the week. Painting the house or stripping some furniture would be considered long-range goals.
- Daydream. Give you mind a chance to relax by pretending you are on a beach or sitting on a blanket in a country meadow.
- Take a nap. This is a good time to catch up on some missed sleep.
- Balance your checkbook. Remember to take the calculator or exercise your mathematical mind and bring scratch paper.
- Update the family budget.
- Do a craft project. This could be knitting, cross-stitch, or needlepoint.
- Read the newspaper.
- Sort through paperwork or the mail.
- Mend clothes, sewing on buttons or hemming a skirt.
- Read school newsletters. Highlights things that will require your action.
- Clean your car with a hand vacuum and damp cloth.
- Use your car phone to make necessary calls. This could negatively affect your household budget if you make peak-time calls.
- Conduct business: Dictate a letter on a tape recorder or balance a budget. I spend my time writing columns for Domestic Planner.
- Read to younger children or play word games with them.

- Listen to your favorite music.
- Think of something you have never done before. Write down a plan to make it happen.
- Plan to do nothing! Your body and mind can always use a ten-minute break.

We seem to spend months of our lives in checkout lines. Use this time to make lists; a list for Christmas or birthday gifts, a list of people to call or errands to run.

How many times have you waited while on the telephone? We make a call and hear a lengthy recorded message before a live voice is heard. Use a portable phone and be prepared to do something while you wait. If you are at the office, do some filing. If you are at home, fold a load of laundry. Make sure you are ready to respond when someone says, 'Hello may I help you!' One afternoon I was waiting on hold to place a product order. I left my order form on the desk and went to the other end of the house to fold laundry. I had to scramble back to my office when I suddenly heard the voice on my portable phone ask, 'May I take your order?'

Today's Refrigerator Bulletin:
  "Organize your wait and reap the benefits!"

Bedtime

Q: I intend to go to bed at a decent hour but household chores demand my immediate attention. I have so much to do and not enough time to get it all done.

A: At the end of the day, we realize everything we wanted to get done is still staring us in the face. The following is a common scenario.

- It is 11:00 P.M. and I am tired and ready for bed.
- I tell my husband I will meet him shortly after I do a couple things.
- I had better start the children's lunches.
- What should I fix for dinner tomorrow? I will be gone the entire day.
- Let me load the dishes in the dishwasher.
- I guess I need to unload the clean dishes first.
- I need to look over the grocery list and put it in my purse.
- As I glance at the calendar I realize my Grandmother's birthday is tomorrow. I'd better hunt for a card and get it in the mail so it will be only one day late. Where was that last stamp I had in the drawer?
- I need to put the school bags by the door and check each bag for a parent note.

- On no, I forgot Amanda is going on a field trip and she needs a special sack lunch, a signed note, and $2.00.
- I'd better glance at today's mail in case there is something important.
- I begin to tackle the paper stack on the counter and realize it is an impossible task. I need a larger block of time for such a project.
- I walk through the family room and see everyone's clutter. I pick up a few items.
- As I head down the hallway I begin to pick up a trail of dirty clothes.
- I stop by the laundry room to fold the forgotten laundry in the dryer and dry the load in the washer.
- I am really getting tired.
- The dress I need to wear for tomorrow's appointment needs ironing.
- Who left the wet towels on the bathroom floor?
- As I go to kiss my toddler good night I trip over the toys on the floor. I do a quick toy pick-up.
- I forgot to check my e-mail and I am expecting some important information for tomorrow's meeting.
- I wonder if someone fed the dog today? He looks hungry.
- I put on my gown, wash my face, and brush my teeth and floss.
- I really should take time to do my nails so they are nice for my appointment.
- Let me make sure all the doors are locked.
- I do not remember if I prepared the coffeepot for morning breakfast.
- I finally crawl into bed next to my snoring husband.
- I look at the clock and it is 1:00 A.M.
- As I close my eyes I realize I am exhausted and the next day has already begun.

Does this describe the end of your day? If so, you need a new plan. Outline a plan for preventing each of these setbacks. Here are some hints. You should implement a regular cleaning schedule, enlist the help of all family members, train them, and create a place for everything in your house. Good luck!

Today's Refrigerator Bulletin:
"It is time for a new plan!"

New Year's Resolutions

Q: **Every year I make New Year's Resolutions to keep my house neat, lose weight, and spend more time with my family. By the end of January I become discouraged at my lack of progress. Should I even bother to make the list this year?**

A: Fulfilling your New Year's Resolutions will require organization and discipline in thought and action. It is an exciting moment in time to experience a new year but you need to be realistic when you make a commitment to change something in your life. First, decide what you want to change, and then think about how your life would be improved by the change. Next, make a plan to execute the change. Finally, put your plan in action.

Steps you can take to succeed in your New Year's Resolutions:

- Start with a clean slate. Do not dwell on past failures but look towards future successes.

- Make a written list of your resolutions. Prioritize your list by putting the most important changes at the top of the list. Place the written list in a location to which you can refer on a daily basis.

- Write a plan to accomplish each item on your list of resolutions. Say you want to lose weight; you need a plan if you are going to accomplish that goal. There are hundreds of approaches you could take but choose one that you feel has the best chance of succeeding. Join a weight loss organization, work with a friend who shares the same goal, use books, diet programs, or consult a physician.

- Find a pacing partner to check your progress. Make sure this person has a copy of your list and understands your goals.

- Record your progress in a notebook. When you achieve success in an area put a star sticker beside the resolution. Make a notation to yourself that says, 'Great job, keep up the good work.' Children need lots of pats on the back but so do adults.

- Be prepared to fail but do not let failure discourage you. Live by the motto, 'If at first you don't succeed, try, try again.' Never give up and you will find success.

- Look at the small picture so you do not become overwhelmed. If your plan for January is to have a clutter-free house then make a plan to tackle each room one at a time. Remove the clutter and maintain a clutter-free atmosphere in that room before moving to the next room. If you tackle the entire house at once you may easily become discouraged.

- Make realistic resolutions. Yes, it is okay to make a couple unrealistic resolutions: that is the stuff dreams are made of. But concentrate on the ones you can actually realize.

- Make sure the success of your resolutions is only dependent on you, not on another person or a machine. You can only control your actions, not someone else's.

- Plan a celebration when you successfully achieve one of your resolutions. A celebration might include a night out to dinner or a new outfit.

- Include on your 'Year List' some new family traditions.

- Take photos at the close of the year; preserve your pictures in photo safe albums. Collect and preserve other memorabilia.

Time disappears daily from our schedule. Schedule your time wisely and be a good steward of your time. You are in control of your time destiny. Make a plan and put action to your plan. Happy New Year!!!

Today's Refrigerator Bulletin:
  "Start the Year with a successful plan to change!"

Closets
Drawers

Crammed Clothes

Q: I need more space in my dresser drawers and closet. Whenever I straighten my clothes they get messy and out of order within a few days.

A: Space for things is a continual problem if we do not have a workable organization system. Clothes take up a lot of space. We tend to accumulate clothes quicker than we get rid of them. We all have clothing items that do not fit or that we rarely wear. Often, we keep these clothes 'just in case' we can wear them again. These extra clothing items end up stuffed in our drawers and crammed into our closets. It is difficult to find the outfit you want to wear if you have to sort through many other articles of clothing. This continuing battle can be won if you create a system to help resolve this problem. Make your accommodations fit your needs. Periodically evaluate your system as you discover better ways to organize.

Tips for Organizing Clothes

- Sort through each article of clothing and decide to keep or remove it from your closet. If there are items you have not worn in a long time but are not ready to part with, put the clothing in a box and store it in the basement. You can make a decision on these items at a later time. Meanwhile they do not take up valuable closet space.

- Ideally, I do not like my hanging clothes to touch each other in the closet. This is not just a neurotic fantasy. When clothes are bunched together in a closet, they wrinkle.

- Arrange 'like' clothing together. You can access a dress quickly with this system. You do not have to hunt through all of your clothes to find a specific dress. You can just look through the section in your closet where the dresses hang.

- You could use dressers with small drawers because they are easier to maintain. If your dresser has large drawers, add small plastic containers to separate items. Neatly fold everything in the drawers and put 'like' items together. You open drawers daily to get clothing items out or to put clean clothes back. Use this time to maintain order by straightening anything out of place. It takes less time to maintain than reorganize the entire drawer. The drawer should close easily without clothes getting stuck. If the drawer does not close, it is time to reorganize.

- You should separate socks by color and style into plastic containers in the dresser drawers. Put white socks in one basket and dark socks in another. When you divide items, you conquer the messy problem.

- Your children can help you neatly organize their closet and drawers. If they know everything has a place and where each item belongs they will be able to maintain order in their room.

- You can purchase plastic drawer containers from your local discount store. Use these in closets for extra drawer space. They are ideal for socks, stockings, tights, handkerchiefs, and underclothing.

- Store shoes in the original box on the floor of your closets or on shoe racks.

- Purchase containers with several dividers for small items such as barrettes, watches, and jewelry.

- I clip bows on a long ribbon I have attached to a hanger in the closet so they do not take up drawer space. I hang hair ribbons from a hanger so they will not wrinkle and I will be able to find the one I want.

- If you have limited space you can purchase containers for under the bed storage.

- Allow for extra space in each drawer and closet. It will be easier to access items and there will be room for additional items.

- You can rotate seasonal clothes from bedroom closets to a basement closet or less accessible storage area. I store off-season clothes in two dressers in the basement.

Avoid Crammed Clothes in the Following Ways:

- Divide clothes into separate compartments
- Do not overcrowd dressers and closet
- Put like clothing articles together

Today's Refrigerator Bulletin:
"Separate clothing and keep drawers and closets partly empty!"

Full Closet

Q: I have a walk-in closet in my bedroom that is too full. My closet is stuffed with clothes, shoes, blankets, pillows, mystery boxes and other assorted junk. The worst part is, I can't seem to find anything when I need it. Do you have some suggestions?

A: There are some specific problems associated with walk-in closets. First, they are so big that we tend to drop things in the closet just to get them out of the way. Consider this scenario: Guests are arriving shortly. To get rid of the clutter around your house you toss everything into the walk-in closet. It is a convenient place to stick unfolded laundry, papers, toys, dirty clothes, and even dirty dishes (in an emergency). Of course, the best way to prevent this calamity is to keep order in the rest of the house but let's deal with that troublesome closet right now. We must treat that closet like a 'special storeroom' with a stern, uncompromising gate-keeper. As we bring things into the closet, we must get them past this gate-keeper. He knows exactly what should be stored in his closet and he allows only those things to pass. All the rest, he turns away with the words, "This has no place in my closet." Obviously, the rejected items go somewhere else. We must determine where they go and put them there. It is important to 'install' a gate-keeper just inside the door of each of your closets.

This alone, won't solve all your problems however. Your imaginary gate-keeper may keep undesirable things out but you already have an incredible mess inside the closet. This requires an intense Closet Investigation. Ask yourself the question, "Do I use everything in my closet and how often is it used?" The answer to these two questions will decide the fate of each item in the closet. Start by preparing a box for items to be given away. Things never used and not needed should be put in this box. Some items that fall into this category are hard to part with simply because we have a sentimental attachment to the items. It helps to prepare a 'sentimental' box for these articles. Go through this box once or twice a year to see if emotional attachment toward any of the items has diminished. Everything that does not go into the 'give away' box or the 'sentimental' box should be categorized as used either yearly, monthly, weekly, or daily. Items used once a year should be removed from the closet or placed high and in the back of the closet. Articles used monthly should also be put in spaces that are harder to reach. Arrange daily and weekly items in a convenient place. They should be low and in front so other things do not have to be moved around to access them.

Moving things around to look for other things takes time and creates organization problems. We tend to look at our walk-in closet as more space to fill with our treasured possessions. People tend to fill all empty space. Fight this tendency of human nature with all of your might. Don't cram something into every available space. If you do, you will have to completely rearrange your closet every time you bring a new article into it. Instead, leave empty spaces for some of those future 'treasures'.

There are several advantages to following these suggestions, and the results will amaze you.

- Your closet will have a neat and orderly appearance
- You will be able to find items quickly

- What you give away will profit someone else

Today's Refrigerator Bulletin:
"A partially empty closet is a happy closet!"

Drawers and Cabinets

Q: How do I keep my drawers and cabinets organized? Arranging them is a continuous process because they do not stay in order.

A: I understand and have experienced the same dilemma. There are areas in your house that constantly become disorganized within a short amount of time. Study the areas that stay organized and the ones that do not. There are reasons for these phenomena. One reason a drawer or cabinet stays straight for a long period of time is that it is seldom used by members of your household. Another, more desirable reason an area may stay organized is that you have discovered a system that works.

Use a system that requires **dividing into many compartments**. The more you divide, the less likely things will be out of their original place. Add containers to your drawers and cabinets. Purchase plastic containers when you find them on sale. Buy them with lids and without lids. You may not necessarily buy a container knowing what you will do with it, but keep a supply available. Store them in your basement or garage. You will find a use for them at some point in time. It is efficient to have several different kinds and sizes available at all times so you do not have to run to the store in the middle of an organization project.

Let's organize a drawer. I will use my junk drawer as an example. It measures 14 inches in width, 19 1/2 inches in length and 3 inches in height. This is a drawer that contains the following items: pencils, pens, scissors, stapler, staples, rulers, rubber bands, paper clips, calculator, stamps, return address stamp, scotch tape, masking tape, glue, hole punch, string, and tape measure. This drawer used to be a constant source of irritation to me because it was always a mess. I open this drawer without dread now because I have 'divided and conquered.' To 'divide,' or separate items I bought containers. I have four different sized rectangular plastic containers. These are utensil and cosmetic containers that can be purchased at any discount store. I also purchased small round containers. Use your own judgment about which containers to purchase depending on the items you will need to separate. The round containers are for paper clips and rubber bands. I put my pencils and pens together in one container, placing rubber bands around the ones I want grouped together. Another container holds the string, tapes, and glue. The next container has scissors, stapler, staples, hole punch and tape measure. The last container holds the calculator, stamps, and return address stamp. The ruler lies outside the containers against the side of the drawer. I still call it my junk drawer because there is a lot of junk in it, not because it is junked up. It is organized and maintains organization even though five other people use it.

It is also important that you **avoid packing every area totally full**. Every space needs room for growth because we always accumulate items more quickly than we purge useless ones. Suppose, for example, there is a great sale on rubber bands and you decide to stock up. You would not want to put all the rubber bands in the junk drawer because it would become crowded. Store extra rubber bands somewhere else, like on a 'supply' shelf in the basement, until you need to refill the container in the junk drawer.

You will experience victory in the area of drawer and cabinet organization if you follow a simple rule: **Keep things organized for yourself and not others.** I would like to share a story about one of my sons: One day I had worked hard in his room organizing the clothes in his closet and drawers. When he came home from school I was eager to show him how neat everything was. I was a little disappointed when he was not impressed with my efforts. When he saw my disappointment he said, "Cool Mom." At that point I asked him to organize his night stand drawer because I was not sure what to do with everything. He responded, "No one sees it Mom. Why do I have to?" I explained to him that when I have a mess on my hands, I want it clean for myself and not to impress other people. I am not sure he had a total grasp of this concept but I hope in time he will. Despite his comments, I know he is learning and developing organization skills that will benefit him later in life. In order to keep things really organized you have to be self motivated, not crisis motivated or driven by what others may think.

Drawer & Cabinet Tips
- Separate into plastic containers
- Keep some empty space
- Organize for yourself

Today's Refrigerator Bulletin:
"Separate into compartments!"

Seasonal Items

Q: How do I organize things like coats, hats, gloves, swimming items, and other things we do not use year round?

A: Let's start with a system to organize winter items. The number of people in your family and the climate you live in will determine how many outer clothing articles you own. It is important that you have enough storage space and that you have a system that requires low maintenance. Low maintenance means dividing items into categories and training everyone to put items back where they belong.

Create a place for every item:

- Store heavy coats and jackets in a closet. Another option is to mount hooks in a garage or mudroom.

- Purchase a laundry basket in which to store boots. Everyone will be able to locate his boots quickly when a snowstorm comes. Keep the basket in a mudroom or on a closet floor.

- You will need several containers so you can put 'like items' together. Place gloves, mittens, hats, scarves, and neck warmers in separate baskets. To avoid losing gloves, clothespin mates together as you take them off and put them in their basket. Clip the clothespin onto the rim of the basket when the gloves are in use. Put the baskets in a convenient location such as the closet floor or a shelf. You may substitute boxes for baskets to separate items.

- A vinyl shoe rack can also be used to store small articles because it has many compartments for separating items. Hang this rack on a wall or the back of a door.

- Separating articles and placing them in plastic grocery bags that hang from hooks provides a very inexpensive storage method.

- Convenient locations for gloves and hats include coat pockets or sleeves.

- During warmer months store winter items in the basement or the attic. Place coats on hangers in a plastic garment bag or in a basement closet. Protect your wool clothing with moth treatment.
- Young children will need to be able to reach their coats easily so use low hooks and avoid hangers until children are old enough to put their coats on hangers and hang them in the closet. Show them where to put their hats and mittens when they remove them. You can make a game out of organizing their items into the baskets so they will think it is fun to put things in the proper place. Put two baskets on the closet floor, one for mittens and one for hats. Tell you child to toss his hat into the correct container.

Use the same system with summer items as winter clothing. Summer items include beach, swimming, and picnic supplies.

Group items by category, placing each group in a separate container:

- Put beach balls, goggles, and blow-up tubes in one container.

- Put pool shoes in a small basket located in your garage.

- Purchase a plastic or canvas handled bag for beach or pool items. Keep it packed with beach towels suntan lotion, sunglasses, and a change purse with coins for snacks.

- Gather together items needed for a picnic and store them together. You will need a small cooler and picnic basket. Fill the picnic basket with the following items; tablecloth, plastic plates, cups, utensils, napkins, salt, and pepper. You will be ready for a picnic at a minute's notice.

The shelf or closet space you designate in your basement for winter items can also be used for summer items. Simply rotate winter and summer items from the shelf or closet. Put items upstairs when they are in season. Place summer items on a shelf in your garage during the warm season. Winter things will need to be kept inside.

Today's Refrigerator Bulletin:
   "In season or off season, organize all your extra items!"

Basement
Garage
Outside

Basement Organization

Q: **The items we7 do not use daily end up in our basement. My basement is piled with lots of things. I organize it and in a short period of time it ends up cluttered. Any suggestions?**

A: Basements are a great place to store the 'extra' items in our homes. The basement is also a place to accumulate unnecessary junk. Moving from one house to another is the best way I have found to clean out the basement and get rid of things. I usually fight an inward battle when faced with the decision, 'Do I want to keep this or give it away?' I am sentimentally attached to most of my possessions but I am also an organizer. Holding on to items and clearing out clutter are two diametrically opposing forces. An organizer does not keep unnecessary items that add clutter to her home. It is usually easier to part with items that you can sell or give to someone.

All storage spaces, regardless of size, will become cluttered if not carefully managed. My basement is very large and can store a lot of things. Even though I reorganize and remove items several times a year, my large basement still gets cluttered. One day I counted the stuffed toys and decided I could open my own store because we had so many 'like new' toys. My children could play with a different stuffed toy each day for six months. With the help of my children we sorted through the stuffed toys.

We kept some and donated the rest to an organization providing Christmas toys for the needy.

Successful basement organization takes planning. Purchase an abundant supply of plastic containers in many shapes and sizes as you find them on sale. I prefer the 'clear' plastic containers. Save cardboard boxes. If you have space, build wooden shelves in different areas of your basement. Use the system 'divide and conquer' when organizing and maintaining your basement. Divide everything by putting 'like items' together in containers and areas. You can conquer by maintaining this system.

<u>How the system works</u>

Items in smaller storage areas:
If you have children, set aside a very large shelf area to keep toys. Try to keep things in the original box or a clear plastic container. Each child can have his own shelf. If two children are close in age and share toys, you can combine them in a single storage area. Put toys for the younger children on lower shelves. You can also designate shelves for board games that are shared by the entire family.

- Reserve a shelf area for all your holiday decorations. Separate holidays by containers. Exchange the usual decorations in your home for the holiday decorations by trading in and out of the storage boxes.
- Maintain shelves for empty boxes. On one shelf you can stack gift boxes of all sizes. It gives you a complete selection when you need to box and wrap a present. Another shelf can hold boxes belonging to electronics and appliances you have purchased. You should keep the box and sales receipts together until the warranty expires. This will enable you to exchange an item if it breaks.

Items in larger storage areas:
- In larger rooms you can keep a variety of items such as school supplies, gifts, pantry items, old house decor, records, tapes, old year books, travel information, etc. Label each box or container with a number and a color. Each color represents a category. For example, all the boxes with orange labels could contain household items. Create a master list, a list of all items contained in each coded box.
- Use the space under steps for large items such as chairs and tables.
- Keep a metal or plastic shelf unit for tools, screws, nails, flashlights, and other hardware. Separate items into individual containers.
- Store paint cans, varnish, putty, and sealers on utility shelves.

Open areas in my basement:
- Book lovers face some unique organization problems. Even when they use a book only occasionally, they want to be able to find it quickly. If you have lots of books, organize books by categories (subject, content, who uses the book the most). You can build shelves in open areas of the basement for dated or less-used books. You can keep children's books in their play area. Out-dated or never-used books should go into the garage sale or donation box.
- Keep off-season clothes in spare closets or old dressers in the basement. You may want to keep a box for each of your children's sentimental clothing items from their earlier years.

Today's Refrigerator Bulletin:
"Clear out and separate basement items!"

Groomed Yard

Q: I spend most of my time keeping my house clean and organized. How do I find time to do yard work?

A: I use the same system, with necessary modifications, whether I am working in the yard or in the house. Just as I maintain my home by keeping clutter at a minimum I can also maintain my flowerbeds by pulling weeds as they appear. An organized home is not limited to the inside of the house. To be honest, I would rather reorganize a drawer than pull weeds from my flowerbeds, but having an organized and attractive yard is equally important to me.

One way to have an attractive yard is to hire out all or some of the work. This is workable if you have a household budget to accommodate paying for yard work. Most of us have to do the yard work ourselves. You may want to pay for mulch delivery and spreading, or pay for a lawn service. If your sons happen to run a part-time grass cutting business like mine do, you could hire them to mow your lawn.

Schedule yard work on a regular basis just as you schedule cleaning your house. You can work by yourself in the yard, but you may want to consider scheduling yard work as a Saturday family project. Allow more time for yard work during seasonal changes, when you have to tackle bigger projects such as mulching, covering the rose bushes, trenching, and planting.

As your family grows, so do your commitments. Inversely, your free time shrinks. You may want to change your landscaping accordingly. Exchange high yard maintenance for low yard maintenance whenever possible.

Tips for low yard maintenance:

- Spread the mulch thick. This will limit the amount of time spent pulling weeds.

- Plant bushes that do not require trimming.

- Plant hearty flowers that will not need daily watering and can stand up to adverse conditions.

- Dig a deep trench around mulch areas to keep grass and weeds from entering the area.

- Build framed, raised beds to keep weeds and grass out of the flowers.

- Plant perennials instead of annuals.

- Use an electric edger and electric (or gas) weed eater. This gives the yard a finished look with minimum effort.

- Install automatic sprinkler system. This obviously reduces the need for manual watering.

It is important to educate yourself in the area of yard work. Check at your local nursery or buy books about plant and lawn care. Determine how much time you can devote to yard work and then decide which plants to buy. Maintaining healthy trees, bushes, and plants requires more than digging a hole. I learned the importance of yard education when we hired a company to landscape. After the estimate I realized we could purchase a new dining room set and still have the yard landscaped if we did the work ourselves. I decided that anyone could dig a hole. Labor Day weekend the nursery delivered 100 trees & bushes and 50 bags of mulch. I realized quickly that Plan A was not going to work. My husband, three small children and I could not possibly plant 100 trees and bushes in three days. Plan B went into immediate action, despite the fact that I really didn't have a Plan B. Friends, neighbors and relatives offered help, and by the evening of the third day the yard looked professionally landscaped.

Today's Refrigerator Bulletin:
   "Organize your home inside and outside!"

Tackling the Garage

Q: There is not enough room for my car and all the other things in my garage. How do I organize my garage to make room for everything?

A: The garage is a great invention. You can park your car, and unload groceries. If the weather is rainy you are safe from the elements and on icy, snowy mornings you do not have to scrape the windshield. Just as important, a garage also serves as a storage bin for many household items.

The garage and the basement are great places to put those things we do not know what else to do with. Unfortunately, they quickly become a cluttered mess. I have made it my mission not to fall prey to that trap. I avoid this in two ways: I 'spring clean' my garage several times a year. I neatly arrange items by separating into areas and containers.

When I pull my car into the garage I want to be able to open my door without hitting a bike, trash can, or lawn mower. My garage is never as organized as I would like it to be, but I continually work towards my goal. Our garage is packed to capacity even though I purge it thoroughly several times a year. I stand in the garage and look around to see what I can remove. This is what I see: Things belonging to four children, items my husband likes to keep in case he needs them in the future, two lawn mowers for my sons' grass cutting business, a snow shovel for each family member, two cars, bikes, trash cans, wheelbarrow, gardening supplies, hoes, tools, rakes, etc. The list is endless. I have concluded we need to build a shed in the back yard but until that happens I have come up with some organizational ideas that have helped make my garage efficient.

Tips for Garage Organization

1. My husband attached two long pegs above the back door on which to hang lawn chairs. We can easily hang eight chairs on the pegs. The chairs used to stand up against the wall of the garage which made it hard to open car doors or sweep the garage floor.

2. We extended the back of our garage and included a sink, shelf and extra floor space. The children's bikes are in the extra space. Bikes can also be hung from the rafters during winter months.

3. I like to keep as many items off the garage floor as possible so I can sweep and mop it twice a month. This keeps dirt from blowing into my home. I have several throw rugs at the door opening into the house.

4. Some of our walls are finished and some are bare studs. We put slats of wood across the studs to create bins for baseball bats, rakes, shovels, and tomato stakes.

5. I have hammered nails into the studs to hang saws, snow shovels, bicycle helmets, and certain other articles.

6. The ladders hang on large metal hooks that are attached to the studs.

7. Above the sink is a shelf holding a container with extension cords, a bucket with cleaning supplies, etc.

8. It is also handy to have several shelves in the garage. Divide everything into storage containers and put 'like items' together on shelves. I separate the children's things into laundry baskets. There is a basket for water guns, large sports balls, small balls and baseball gloves. The tennis rackets are stacked on a shelf together. There is a handled basket for gardening tools. Weed killer, plant food, and bags of fertilizer are in an open plastic container. Fishing equipment is also in this area. Smaller containers are used for dog supplies, tools, flashlights, nails & screws, string, and tape.

9. Put up racks with hooks on which to hang coats and school backpacks.

10. Attach hooks for umbrellas, fly swatters, shoe horns, plastic grocery bags, and other items.

11. I have 3 shoe racks (two on the floor and one on the wall), and a basket for shoes. We do not wear shoes in the house so, except for seasonal shoes and dress shoes, we keep them in the garage. I have them separated so everyone has his own specific area.

12. I keep only large items on the garage floor such as trashcans, lawn mowers, bikes, the wheelbarrow, and golf clubs. I can sweep the garage faster if I do not have to spend time moving items.

Today's Refrigerator Bulletin:
    "Organize the BIG space in your garage by separating and putting like items together!"

Car Clutter

Q: My car is constantly cluttered with papers, toys, cans, and cups. How can I consistently keep a neat, clean car?

A: Like many areas of your home the car is an easy target for clutter. We spend a large amount of time in the car, therefore it is part of our daily living space. There are many reasons for a cluttered car. Almost every item in our home enters via the car. In the age of fast foods and a fast pace, the car is also a restaurant on wheels. This tends to leave a legacy of forgotten french fries under seats and behind cushions. Upon returning home from school, lessons, and practices, our kids burst from the car leaving their belongings behind. Of course, we leave things in the car all the time, too.

You need an organized system to maintain a clean, clutter-free car. Train family members to be responsible to take their personal belonging into the house each time they leave the car. You will need to make this a rule using rewards or consequences. Each time you arrive home, empty the car of your personal items and any purchases you have made. Do not be tempted to unload the car and dump items on the kitchen counter. Make sure you put everything away when you get into the house so you do not create another clutter area.

Keep a rotating basket in your car. A rotating basket works similar to the rotating shelves in your home. The rotating basket is a home for temporary items such as wallpaper, library books, or a return item. You need to take the wallpaper to the hardware

173

store in order to match paint colors for your bedroom wall, return the library books to the library, exchange an item at a store. The basket in your car will contain these items so they are not rolling around on the floor. It will also serve as a reminder of errands you must do. Take the basket back and forth from car to house for loading and unloading purposes.

Some items should remain in your car. Keep a plastic trash bag in the car for discarded items. Keep wipes for spills or sticky hands. If your car does not have a built in drink holder you may want to purchase one. For music listeners, a cassette or CD organizer is handy. In the glove box or in a basket under the seat keep car insurance and registration information, a pen, paper, coins for tolls and parking meters, a flashlight, and an ice scraper.

Schedule a time to wash and vacuum your car weekly. There are several options depending on the weather conditions. Wash and vacuum it yourself at home. Fill up with gas and drive through a car wash. There is usually a vacuum facility available. Pay your child or a neighborhood child to clean the car.

Each time you eat in the car prepare for a clean-up when you arrive home. Take trash out to prevent spoiled food odors. Vacuum food crumbs. A hand vacuum will work best. You want to avoid food spills in your car. When you transport prepared food, put the ingredients in sealed containers. Put the food you have cooked in a basket or box lined with old towels. Make sure everything fits tightly and cannot move around. Secure lids to casseroles with rubber bands. You will want to concentrate on your driving rather than catching food spills. Avoid transporting milk products unless the container is tightly sealed.

On one occasion I decided to bring two gallons of hot chocolate home from a school party. My gut feeling was to dump it down the drain at school but I felt that was wasteful. Despite my anxieties about the hot chocolate, my daughter and I arrived home safely in our mini-van. As I turned off the engine, my daughter decided to come to the front of the van, using the plastic container that held the milk as her stepping stool. Due to the temperature of the hot chocolate, the lid caved in sending a tidal wave of sticky brown liquid onto the carpet. I immediately cleaned up the spill but within a week the van was filled with an extremely foul odor. We had the carpets professionally cleaned but the smell remained. For six months we tried numerous things to get rid of the odor. We used car scents, candles, cleaners, odor absorbents and more. Finally, we removed the carpet and hung it on our back fence for several months allowing it to absorb the rain, snow and sun. Moral of the story: Beware of containers bearing milk.

Today's Refrigerator Bulletin:
    "Spend a few extra minutes to empty the car before entering the house!"

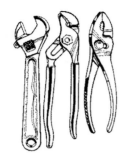

Car Maintenance

Q: What do I do to maintain an efficient, reliable car? How often do I take my car in to be serviced and what is necessary for routine maintenance?

A: It is important to maintain your car by having an organizational plan. Without the use of your car you can not do the errands required to run an efficient household. You also need to act responsibly so as not jeopardize the safety of your family.

Find an auto repair shop that you can trust and is geographically close to your house. Shop around by asking friends and neighbors if they are happy with their mechanic. If you had a medical need you would find the best physician you could. Your mechanic is your car's doctor.

Ask the shop about car maintenance; what should be done and how often. Opinions may vary between auto shops. You should routinely:

- change the motor oil
- check for loose belts
- check brakes
- general check
- wheel alignment

Keep a notebook in the glove compartment of your car to record car maintenance and repairs. Each time you service your car record the following information:

- place you had the work done
- type of service
- cost
- current mileage
- date

Write on your calendar when you need to take your car in to be serviced. Some work requires a mechanic but there are also things you can do. Check your car manual on suggested maintenance. The manufacturer's maintenance schedule will vary depending on the make and model of your vehicle. Also, do the following on a routine basis:

- Each time you drive your car look at the dash for warning signs. Do not ignore flashing lights or gauge needles.
- Check windshield wiper fluid and check the condition of your wipers.
- Check the air in your tires (buy a tire gauge at your local auto parts store).
- Make sure your spare tire has air and you have all the jack gear.
- To protect the paint and prevent rust, immediately remove corrosive materials such as salt, tar, bird droppings, and mud.
- Examine the garage floor or pavement where you usually park for telltale spots that could indicate fluid leaks.
- Check the horn.
- Check fluids such as oil, transmission fluid, and brake fluid.
- Check the water level in the radiator.

- Check the blinkers and headlights.

Today's Refrigerator Bulletin:
   "Take proper care of your home on wheels!"

Entertainment
Parties

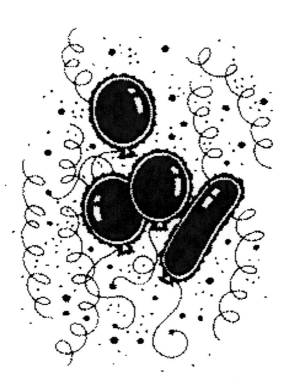

Party Planning

Q: I need some good ideas for planning a party.

A: We all enjoy attending parties but someone has to plan the party, pay for the party, and pick-up after the party is over. Why not have fun planning a party? If you are having a birthday party for one of your children, involve them in the preparations. This not only gives you time to share an important event in his life but it also trains him in the area of organization. If you are planning a party for someone other than your children enlist the help of a friend or relative. You will get twice as much done and enjoy the company of someone else.

Planning the Party:
We have pop-up books; why not a pop-up party? We need to be able to plan a party that is quick and easy. First make a list of everything you need to do. This list would include the theme of the party, invitations, games, food, entertainment, decorations, prizes, clean-up, and thank you notes. After deciding on a theme, purchase (or make) invitations, decorations, prizes, and goodie bags. If you hire entertainment for the party call the organization to schedule the date. Make a guest list and fill out the invitations, mailing them 2 weeks prior to the party. If the party is a surprise, design a plan to make sure the person is

surprised. For children's parties write a schedule of all the activities so you can maintain control. Plan extra activities so if you finish early you will have a contingency. A typical schedule for a 6-year-old's birthday party would include:

10 minutes	Guests arrive, introductions
5 minutes	Group picture
15 minutes	Open the gifts
30 minutes	Entertainment
20 minutes	Sing 'Happy Birthday," refreshments
20 minutes	Games or an art project
10 minutes	Read a story
10 minutes	Hand out goodie bags, good-byes

Remember to capture these special memories with photos and video. Take a group picture to make sure you have a memory of each guest. While your child is opening gifts, write down each gift and whom it is from so you will have accurate records for thank you notes. Each child is given a goodie bag when he leaves. Prizes are awarded for the winners of the games, however for groups of children under the age of seven everyone is given a prize.

Allow plenty of time to shop, prepare food, and decorate. Lay everything out ahead of time such as the camera, video camera, goodie bags, candles, paper goods, refreshments, pad of paper, pen, games, and matches (in your pocket). Prepare a gift table. Clear a place in the closet to hang coats if it is a fall or winter party.

Try to do some clean-up during the party. Have three paper bags available during the gift time for paper trash, bows, cards, and smaller gifts. As each child finishes his refreshments ask him to throw away his plate and cup while you wipe up the table and floor. Try to plan activities in different rooms so your husband, a friend or an older sibling can clean-up the activity from one room as you move to the next room and activity.

Thank you notes are a must in our home because I want to teach my children the importance of being grateful. If someone has taken the time to buy them something they need to thank the person in three ways: when they open the gift, when the person leaves, and with a written note. If they are too young to write then I compose the note as if they wrote it. Once they learn to write I design a basic thank you note on which they just have to fill in the blanks. For example: 'Dear_____, Thank you for the_____. It was nice of you to think of me. Love,_____.' By the time my children are eight they can write their own thank you notes. However, it is my job to either buy the cards on which to write notes or create generic cards on the computer.

Themes for Kids Parties:
Western party, slumber party, sports party, dinner party, dress-up party, tea party, carnival party, beach party, 50's party, ballet party, movie party, and detective party.

Some of the easiest parties for boys are sports parties. You can plan a three-hour party. During the first forty-five minutes open gifts and serve refreshments. The remainder of the time the boys can divide into teams and play an organized game such as soccer. You can watch them from the kitchen window while you clean-up refreshments and take an occasional picture. When the party is over they leave from the backyard and you have a clean house by the time the party is over.

For my oldest daughter's 9th birthday we had a formal dinner party with eight girls. The attire was dress-up in your Sunday best. My husband and I functioned as cooks and waiters. We served a four-course meal on our finest china with the beverage served in crystal. Our daughter was given a dinner bell so we could be summoned. It was a smashing success and the video captured some interesting dinner conversation. We decided to duplicate this party for my youngest daughter's 11th birthday.

Entertainment:
Story teller, magician, clown, and pony rides.

If you are on a limited budget you can be the entertainment instead of hiring entertainers. You can dress as a clown, do a few tricks and handout treats. You will be a smashing hit with young children. My youngest daughter wanted a magician so after checking the cost I bought a magic book and a few supplies. With the help of my older daughter we had ten seven-year-old girls in awe at our performance.

Parties Away from your Home:
Park, pizza place, batting cage, sports complex, bowling, miniature golf, gymnastics, and swimming.

Although I have focused on children's parties, you can use the same basic techniques to plan an anniversary party, adult birthday party, graduation party, baby shower, or wedding shower.

Today's Refrigerator Bulletin:
"The perfect plan is to enjoy the party before, during, and after!"

Party Box

Q: I enjoy entertaining and giving parties but it is so much work I usually hesitate to volunteer as hostess for birthday parties, showers, and other celebrations.

A: You can minimize your workload in planning a party by making a party box. The secret to an easy, successful party is to have the supplies ready ahead of time. Let's start with a basic party box. Your box should be a large clear plastic container with a lid. Label your container 'Party Box.' The party box should include the following supplies:

- Decorative tablecloths, napkins, plates, and cups. Stock your box with generic themes such as floral, balloons, and confetti. You may also want to include baby, wedding, and sports themes.

- Balloons in various sizes and colors.

- Crepe paper in basic primary colors, several pastels, and white.

- Small birthday candles and large decorative candles in various colors. Make sure you store these in a cool environment to prevent them from melting.

- Party banners and flags.

- Invitations either computer-ready or to be hand written.

- Confetti to decorate the counters and table.

- Centerpieces that easily fold flat.

- Party hats and horns.

- Door prizes and party favors (Party favors are not limited to children's parties).

- Music CD's.

- Name tags appropriate for kids or adults.

- String, masking tape, scotch tape, glue, and scissors.

As you create your party box determine the kinds of parties you would be giving. Whenever you are shopping, look for great ideas and good sales on supplies you can buy for your party box. A sachet for the dresser drawer would be an appropriate party favor for the guests at a wedding shower. Kids parties are easy because children enjoy little trinkets that we normally consider 'junk.' Decorative pencils and stickers are also popular with kids. The idea is to have items ahead of time, even before the party is scheduled. This will lighten your load if you have most of the non-perishable items already. You will simply need to invite the guests, prepare snacks, and clean your home. Hire cleaning help the day of your party, and planning a party will be as easy as one, two, three.

Many parties involve gift giving. Make a smaller box and label it 'Gift Wrapping.' This box should contain an assortment of the following supplies: wrapping paper, tissue paper, decorative gift bags, bows, ribbon, tape, and scissors.

You may also choose to create a 'Game Box.' Place in this box a pad of paper, pencils, playing cards, and game idea book. Include several children's traditional games such as 'Pin the Tail on the Donkey,' bean bags, clothespins, and a bottle. There are also many games available for large groups of people of all ages.

You can enjoy entertaining on a routine basis if you start today and prepare your 'Party box.'

Today's Refrigerator Bulletin:
  "Lift off the lid and let the party begin!"

Ladies Luncheon

Q: I would like to have few of my friends over for lunch but I never seem to have enough time to make the arrangements. I would like to use linens and china but maybe I should consider a picnic theme. Something unique would be fun.

A: Often we hesitate to entertain because it consumes too much of our time, money, and energy. Having an organized home and planning ahead will simplify the process of entertaining. Many women spend time cleaning and organizing their home before they can entertain. If you make a plan to deal with clutter on a daily basis and clean your home once a week, it will allow you the freedom to entertain more often.

Now you are ready to plan a luncheon. You can plan a formal luncheon with minimum food preparation or an elaborate affair with more preparation. Use a linen tablecloth, linen napkins, fresh flowers, a scented candle, china, and crystal and your table will look like it has been set for royalty. You can select some beautiful pieces of china inexpensively at antique shops. I spent a summer visiting antique shops and buying china cups, saucers, and luncheon plates. None of the pieces match but altogether they coordinate beautifully on a luncheon table. I also bought a set of clear glass bowls to serve soup or salad. I have used the dishes at several ladies luncheons. It is fun to listen to the comments about how unique each piece is and watch my guests compare the china pieces.

Use paper products for a simplified luncheon. Many stores sell themes such as picnic or beach party with matching napkins, plates, cups, and tablecloths. An alternative to fresh flowers would be to use a silk arrangement as your table centerpiece. You can borrow it from another room in your house that is not in use for the luncheon.

Treat your guests special by putting a scented candle in your bathroom with a single carnation or rose. You could also personalize the luncheon with a name card and a small gift. Write each person's name on folded card stock paper. You can decorate each card with stickers and calligraphy, or use a stencil. Select a simple gift such as a bookmark, small scented candle, or mints wrapped in tulle and tied with a decorative ribbon.

Take a photo of the event. You will not only have a cherished memory but you can also refer to the picture next time you prepare a luncheon. Send a copy of the picture to your guests. They can keep a memory of the special day.

Hire your children to serve the food, clear the table, and clean up the kitchen. You will accomplish three things: you can spend the time with your guests, allow your children to earn spending money, and your guests will be impressed with your little helpers.

A ladies luncheon would not require the same amount of food as a couple's dinner party. Your menu could include something simple like dollar rolls with cheese and deli meat, a fresh fruit or jello salad, and a relish tray. In cooler weather prepare soup in the crockpot. For dessert serve a cookie with ice cream or sherbet. Offer two to three beverages. This could include tea, coffee, soda, or punch.

An alternative menu could be quiche, lettuce salad, and strawberry shortcake for desert. I have included an easy, delicious recipe for Quiche and shortcake.

Quiche
10" unbaked pie shell
6 ounces swiss cheese
8 slices crisp bacon
3 beaten eggs
1 cup heavy cream
1/4 cup milk
1/2 teaspoon salt
1/4 teaspoon pepper
dash of cayenne
1/2 teaspoon dry mustard

Put crumbled bacon and grated cheese in the pie shell. Blend other ingredients and pour into the shell. Bake at 375 degrees for 35-45 minutes.

Excellent Shortcake
3 eggs
1 cup granulated sugar
1/3 cup almost boiling water
1/4 teaspoon vanilla
1 cup flour
dash of salt
1 1/2 teaspoon baking powder

Beat eggs with mixer for five minutes gradually adding sugar. Add water and vanilla and continue to beat for 30 seconds. Sprinkle in flour, salt, and baking powder and continue to beat. Grease and flour an 8-inch pan and bake at 350 degrees for 30 minutes. Serve warm or cool with strawberries and whipped cream.

Today's Refrigerator Bulletin:
"From the oven to your guests' heart!"

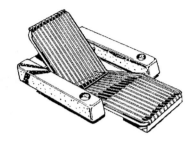

Pool and Patio

Q: How can I prepare for outdoor entertaining. When unannounced guests arrive during the summer months, how can I feed them at a moment's notice without spending hectic hours in the kitchen?

A: The whisper of summer makes us think of sunny skies, warm breezes, pool splashes, and picnics. Use the last month of winter and the first month of spring to prepare for some outdoor fun. Begin by sprucing up the back yard. Plant some grass seed in the bare spots. This will limit the amount of mud that gets tracked into your house during the spring rains. Purchase some hanging plants to display around your patio. You can also plant flowers around the patio area. You will enjoy the atmosphere as you entertain guests on warm summer evenings.

You will want to plan ahead if you intend to buy patio furniture or lawn chairs. If you are on a budget, visit a resale shop or spend a day hitting garage sales. An old quilt provides ideal seating for toddlers and small children. Laundering and storing blankets is easy. Keep chair cushions inside when you are not using them because the sun will quickly damage them.

Clean the barbecue grill and make sure you have plenty of propane or charcoal and lighter fluid. Buy a grill brush to make cleaning up easier, and use it after meal preparation. Covering your grill between uses will protect it from weather, animals, and dirt. Most grill manufacturers also offer tarps and other accessories made specifically to fit your grill. Plan ahead if you need a new barbecue grill so you can purchase it during off-season when they are usually less expensive.

Remove dirt by cleaning the concrete patio with a bleach solution, or rent a power washer. If you keep pets in your yard, power washing is recommended. If you have a deck, stain and seal it early in the season. You can enjoy it for the entire season without worrying about sealing it during the hot summer months. Buy a new door mat to catch outside dirt before it sneaks into your home.

Stock a first aid kit to handle insect stings or bites, cuts, and sunburns. Ways to prevent sunburn include using plenty of sun block or avoiding excess sun exposure by planting shade trees by your patio, buying a large umbrella, or installing a patio tarp or awning. For a fun alternative, keep big hats and sunglasses handy for your guests to use.

Prepare a patio container full of supplies you can use to entertain on short notice. Put the following items in the container; paper or plastic plates & cups, napkins, a tablecloth, salt & pepper, silverware, utensils for grilling, barbecue sauce, ketchup, mustard, and relish. Keep an abundance of hamburger patties, hot dogs, buns, and corn on the cob in the freezer. Keep an extra bag of chips, several cans of baked beans and several brownie mixes on hand throughout the summer months. If you would prefer not to share your meal with the local insects you can buy a food net. This will protect your food while you are waiting to serve. You will instantly be ready for a patio party with minimal work. While your guests are present you will want to spend this valuable time entertaining instead of working in the kitchen.

Whether you own a pool or visit a public facility you will want to make some preparations. As a pool owner you will need a maintenance plan and a safety plan. Accidents happen suddenly and when we least expect them. The area around the pool should be locked at all times unless attended by a responsible adult. Chemicals should also be locked away. Make sure you have the proper equipment and you know CPR. Keep a pool bag packed with towels, sunscreen, goggles, pool toys, coins for buying snacks, sunglasses, and a great book for Mom. This is especially important if you visit a public or subdivision pool, but you can keep a similar bag ready (with slight modifications) for the backyard pool. Instead of coins, for example, include some pre-packaged, heat tolerant snacks. You will also want to keep swimming suits and pool shoes in the bag unless you plan on wearing them to the pool.

Make sure pool items return to the pool bag and patio items return to the patio container. Every item should live in its home so you will not waste time looking for it when guests visit or you load the car to head for the pool.

Today's Refrigerator Bulletin:
"Prepare now and play later!"

Children's Party Games

Q: Could you suggest some party game ideas for children's birthday parties? When are they too old to play party games?

A: You are never too old to play games. Children of all ages (including adults) enjoy age appropriate games. Toddlers and pre-school children enjoy repeating the same games over and over again. Have you ever noticed how long you can play 'peek-a-boo' with a baby? They giggle each time you hide your face as if it were the first. Bridge is a card game you can begin in elementary school and play until you are one hundred. Many games will hit a variety of ages, while an individual age group might play specific games.

Sprinkle in several traditional games with your party planning but also introduce some new games. Traditional games include musical chairs, drop the clothespins in the milk bottle, pin the tail on the donkey, and bean bag toss. You can vary the presentation of these games. Instead of pin the tail on the donkey you could pin the candles on the top of the cake. Drop colored clothespins into the bottles, assigning a different number of points for each color; ten points for blue, five for red, and so on. Musical chairs could be altered to musical candy walk. Use masking tape to mark a circular walking path on the floor. Divide the path into squares, taping a number onto each square. Write each number on a piece of paper and place in a basket. The children march around the squares as the music plays. When the music stops a number is drawn. The child standing on that number chooses a piece of candy.

A home carnival is another option for a birthday party. You will need several adult helpers to supervise the games in each area. Make or buy carnival tickets. You will also need lots of candy and small prizes.

Game ideas:

- Bowling: Arrange 2-liter soda bottles in a triangle and use a small rubber ball.
- Ball toss into a clown mouth
- Guess the amount: Fill a jar with M&M's or chocolate kisses. Record each child's guess. The closest guess wins.
- Birthday toss: Put a large calendar on the floor and decorate the day of your child's birthday. Have children toss pennies and try to land on the correct date.

Give each child a small paper bag to decorate. Write their name and let them decorate with crayons, markers, and stickers. Food ideas include popcorn, ice cream cones, cotton candy, and snow cones. Send everyone home with their prize bag and a balloon. For the final touch, rent or make a clown costume.

Plan relay games for your birthday party if you have adequate space. Form two or more teams depending on the number of children:

- Balloon Pop Relay: The first person on each team runs towards an inflated balloon and sits on it until it pops. The player runs back and tags the next person. Once each team member has popped a balloon the team sits down. The first team to sit down wins.

- Orange Relay: Two people on the same team put an orange between their cheeks and walk to the other side of the room and back. If they drop the orange they must go back to the beginning.
- Penny Relay: Walk or run to the other side of the room with a penny on the top of each shoe. Return to your team and give the next person the pennies.
- Three-leg Relay: Use burlap bags or old king size pillowcases. Two people from each team place one leg in the bag and one leg out, then race to the finish line.
- Ball Relay: The first person on each team places a ball between his knees and hops across the room and back handing the ball to the next person in line.

Game books are also widely available at bookstores and libraries. Don't forget to ask the birthday boy or girl what games he or she would like to play, but be ready with several suggestions.

Today's Refrigerator Bulletin:
   "Play traditional and new games to make your birthday party complete!"

Baby Shower

Q: My best friend is expecting a baby. I want to give her the best baby shower in history. Help me to find the secret.

A: Baby showers do not need to be boring or routine. What an opportunity, to celebrate new life with people you love. Have fun and most of all, be creative. The first myth to dismiss is 'when.' Baby showers can be given either before or after the birth of the baby. If this is the couple's first child, basic supplies will be needed for the layette. If more than one shower is planned, schedule one event after the birth so that you can supply gifts knowing the size and sex of the baby. This shower could also provide an opportunity for mom to show off her new 'bundle of joy.'

Many families today are separated by hundreds of miles, which could make a conventional shower logistically difficult. Instead, plan a mail order shower. Invite family and friends over for a celebration just as if the 'guest of honor' were present. Allow each guest to express a greeting into a video camera. Take photos of the event. Send the wrapped gifts, the video tape, and the developed photos to the mother-to-be.

As hostess of a baby shower you make the decision on the date of the event, whom to invite, the decorations, the food, and the entertainment. Begin by making a guest list and sending out invitations. Include a list of needed gift items in the invitation. Try to avoid a surprise shower. These are fun but not very practical for an expectant mother. She would be relaxed and enjoy the event more if you invited her ahead of time.

Next, you must decide on the decorations. Choose a theme and coordinate the paper goods to match. You can stick with the traditional pastel colors such as blue, pink, and yellow or be daring and use bold primary colors such as red, blue, and bright yellow. If you choose primary colors, you may consider a circus or a zoo theme.

Food preparations can be as simple as cake, nuts, mints and punch. Another possibility is a simple meal. This could include dollar rolls with deli meats & cheeses, chips, lettuce salad, punch, coffee, tea, and cheesecake. Make the decision according to your budget and the time of day.

Party favors are not necessary but they are a nice touch. Cut cardstock paper into a triangle. Fold the three corners together and fasten with a safety pen to form a diaper. Fill the diaper with party mints or mixed nuts.

After the mother-to-be opens gifts, you may want to play games before serving refreshments. If you provide prizes for the winners, your guests will be more eager to play. A few suggestions are listed below:

- Recite the first stanza of a nursery rhyme and have each guest complete the next line on paper.
- See which guest can come up with the most names for the new baby. The first person to write twenty-five names is the winner.
- Give each guest five minutes to make a list of what would be included in a baby layette.

Each guest can choose to bring an individual gift or you could coordinate a group purchase for larger items such as a crib, a stroller, or a high chair. You may want to assign some guests to bring personal gifts for the mother-to-be; lotions, perfume, scented soaps, or a coupon to a nearby hotel (the new mom and dad may need a get-away night a few months after the birth). Instead of the traditional baby gifts consider buying disposable gifts such as diapers, lotion, shampoo, cotton swabs, and cotton balls. This is particularly appropriate if the couple has other children and may already own some of the bigger items.

A new baby turns the household routine upside down. Such simple tasks as eating, sleeping, and maintaining a clean, tidy house are threatened. Anticipating this, use the shower as an opportunity to provide solutions for the expectant mother. Ask the guests to fill out coupons for promised services and present them to the mother-to-be. Some examples of these services include the following:

- Prepare and deliver a meal to the family. Use disposable dishes so that no one has to remember to return anything.
- Take siblings on an outing for the day. This will allow the new mom to spend time with the baby or catch up on lost sleep.
- Help with housework and laundry.
- Offer to baby-sit so mom and dad can have a date night.

The new arrival can make life difficult for a toddler or pre-school child. Invite the sibling to the shower and buy a special gift for him (or her) because he is the big brother or sister. The gift doesn't need to be elaborate: A coloring book and crayons or a toy will do nicely.

Today's Refrigerator Bulletin:
"Plan a special event to welcome someone new to the world!"

Bridal Shower

Q: My friend's wedding is fast approaching and I would like to plan a bridal shower for her. Do you have some unique suggestions?

A: Many types of showers can be plan for either the bride-to-be or for the engaged couple. Begin with a few basics. Decide on a budget and how much time you can devote to party preparations. These considerations will determine what kind of shower you will arrange. The next step is to make a guest list and schedule a date and time for the event. Select a theme for the shower (some suggestions are listed below), choose decorations, and plan the menu. Mail out the invitations at just the right time: Two weeks prior to the shower is appropriate. You want to give people enough time to respond but not so much time that they forget to attend. Include other important information in the invitation: Is it a surprise, is a meal planned, is the couple registered at a specific retail store?

On the day of the shower provide each guest with a name tag unless it is a group of established friends. Make sure everyone feels included. Have each guest state her name, and her relationship to the bride or groom. Seat the guest of honor so that all other guests have a clear view while she opens the gifts. Assign one person to record the gift and giver. Have someone else collect wrapping paper and bows. Take photos of this memorable event so in future years each moment can be relived.

Bridal Shower ideas:

- For the busy hostess, plan a simple but elegant shower at a restaurant.

- There will be times in which a 'money tree shower' would be appropriate. One instance would be if the couple was moving overseas, making it costly to transport gifts. In the case of a second marriage, the couple may already have the basics to set up house. Have each guest bring a card with money. Use a small artificial Christmas tree (without the Christmas decorations) to display the cards.

- Choose a houseware theme in which each guest brings something for the home. Along with a gift, tell everyone to bring one disposable household item. Offer suggestions such as dish soap, laundry soap, tissue boxes, and toilet paper. The cost per individual would be slight, but it would result in great savings for a new couple on a limited budget. Ask each guest to drop the disposable item into a large laundry basket you have placed near the front door. Present the basket to the bride when she is finished opening her gifts and tell her this is a bonus from all her guests.

- A personal shower is fun to give with close friends and family. The gifts would include lingerie, perfume, and bath and body lotions.

- Give a shower in which each guest brings a handmade item. This idea works well if the guests are involved in craft clubs. If a member of a quilting club is getting married the group could surprise her with a handmade quilt and a joint gift.

- Have a 'cook it up special' shower. Mail a blank recipe card to each guest. Ask each guest to write her favorite recipe on the card and actually prepare and bring the dish. Your food preparations are complete and the guest of honor can sample each recipe. Call each guest to see what she is bringing so you do not end up with ten desserts and zero main dishes.

- Plan an afternoon 'tea party.' Decorate with elegant linen, china, and fresh flowers. Serve dollar rolls spread with chicken salad, fresh fruit, cheesecake, and assorted teas.

- 'Around the clock party' is fun for the bride-to-be and each guest. Include in each person's invitation a specific hour of the day or night and ask her to bring a gift associated with that hour. You may need to coordinate some of the gifts so that the people assigned morning hours do not all bring coffee pots.

- Start the new bride off with a variety of spices by planning a 'spice shower.' Assign each guest a spice to bring in addition to her other gift. Buy a wall spice rack or a carousel spice rack in which to store the spices.

- Awarding prizes or party favors are a nice touch. You can play games for prizes or simply award door prizes by marking the bottom of the dessert plates or drawing names from a basket.

- A 'couples' dinner party is an excellent way to include the groom-to-be. Add a little fun to the party by asking each guest to write down advice about marriage and present it to the couple. During the dinner, the host can ask each attendee questions requiring a response, such as: What has been a high point in your relationship? If you could have a fantasy trip together where would you go? Name one thing your partner does for you that you enjoy. How did you meet? Why did you decide to get married?

Today's Refrigerator Bulletin:
"Choose the perfect celebration for the bride-to be!"

Family
Activities

Affordable Entertainment

Q: Our household budget is tight. What kind of inexpensive family activities can I plan?

A: With creative planning you can minimize the amount of money spent on entertainment. A substantial portion of our income is spent on pleasure in today's society. Even in two income families it can be difficult to maintain a high standard of living while indulging in frequent recreation. A movie and dinner for two put extra pressure on the family budget.

In order to work within a budget, you must first examine the activities you currently enjoy. If your primary source of recreation is even moderately expensive, consider trying something new. People are reluctant to try new things, yet many times when we make changes we are pleasantly surprised at the results.

Decide how much money you will spend on entertainment. On pay day put the budgeted money in two envelopes labeled 'entertainment,' one for the entire family and one for you and your spouse. Whether you choose a variety of activities or focus on a specific area, you should try to accommodate the tastes of everyone in the family. This usually requires some compromise. Favorite activities may fall into one of the following categories; fine arts, sporting events, physical activities, social activities, intellectual activities. Try to include both indoor and outdoor activities (weather permitting). Do not spend more than you have set aside in the envelopes.

After identifying your areas of interest, spend time scouting for coupons and free admissions. Look for coupons in the mail or your local newspaper. The radio announces events and discounts. Inquire at your local City Hall or Chamber of Commerce for upcoming events in your area. Purchasing a membership or season pass to popular local attractions is worth while if you plan to attend the activity multiple times. Many cultural, educational, and entertainment venues offer free or discounted admissions on specific days. Others are always free but require reservations. Investigate the possibilities! If you plan ahead, you should rarely have to pay full price for any activity. Establishments that want your business usually offer incentives.

Arrange for a family meeting to discuss entertainment options. Give your family choices after you have gathered the information. Compare everyone's schedule and then take a family vote. Write on your calendar the place, time and cost of your social event.

Inexpensive Entertainment Ideas:

<u>**Fine Arts:**</u>
- Visit the museums in your area.
- Some outdoor musical theater venues offer discounted or free seats.
- During the warmer months, look for free concerts in the park.
- Performances of church or high school choirs are usually free.
- View educational television shows on the arts.
- Rent a movie at your local video store. Wait for the one dollar rental instead of paying for a new release.
- Plays performed at high schools or colleges are inexpensive yet often are more entertaining than the professional versions.

<u>**Sporting Events:**</u>
- Attend professional sporting events and sit in the inexpensive seats or take advantage of free or discounted promotional tickets offered by businesses or with products.
- Attending a high school or college game can be fun and inexpensive.

<u>**Physical Activities:**</u>
- Hike on trails or strike your own path through the woods. Make sure you are not trespassing.
- Go swimming.
- Sign up for a volleyball, softball, basketball, or soccer league. If team sports leagues are not available in you area, help organize one.
- Use coupons for sports that cost money such as golf, skiing, bowling, miniature golf, amusement parks, etc. Remember gift certificates for your favorite sports

activity when you write birthday or Christmas suggestions.

Social Activities:
- Look for 'buy one - get one free' restaurant coupons.
- Arrange for a game night with friends and ask everyone to bring a snack to share.
- Plan a potluck dinner where each guest brings food to share.
- Join a church or club. Many of the planned activities are free.
- Volunteer in an area of your interest. Besides meeting new people, you will get to do something you like for free.
- Progressive dinners are fun. Eat each course of the meal at a different house.
- Join a 'game' group that meets regularly to play bridge, bunco, or pinochle.
- Take a picnic lunch to a park.

Intellectual Activities:
- Check the library for chess clubs or literary societies.
- Read a book on a park bench.
- Attend free lectures at churches and universities.
- Enjoy a poetry reading at a coffee house. Better yet, bring something to contribute.
- Join a discussion group.
- Get involved with the local historical society.

Today's Refrigerator Bulletin:
"The best entertainment is spending time with the people you love, not spending a lot of money!"

<u>Vacation</u>

Q: Going on vacation is a lot of work. The following thoughts run through my mind as I pull out of the driveway: "I don't remember if I packed my swimming suit. Did I lock the back door? I think I turned off the iron but I'm not sure." I am exhausted by the time we leave on our trip. It takes days to recover when we return home. Do you have a solution?

A: Organization is a necessary ingredient when preparing for vacation. I plan ahead and keep several written lists. I keep a list of things to do, people to call, items to pack, vacation agenda, and unpacking at home. Every family member has jobs to do. For example; older children can do their own packing, help load the car, be responsible for their own belongings, and assist in vacation planning.

Things to do:
Begin preparing a week before you leave. Make a list of things to buy. Shop for toiletry items, clothing, reading materials, and snacks. Get out the luggage and make sure it is adequate. Gather phone numbers in case of an emergency and addresses to which you may want to send postcards. Put a hold on the mail at the post office or pay a neighbor child to collect your mail while you are gone.

People to Call:

First decide the vacation location and then make the arrangements. We make arrangements months or weeks ahead depending on the destination. It is important to make reservations early to take advantage of discounts. First, make reservations with the airline if you are flying and then reserve the rooms. Call a friend or neighbor to watch the house, feed the dogs and bring in the paper. Leave hotel phone numbers with relatives and friends. As soon as you arrive at your vacation destination, call and make arrangements for tours and other sightseeing trips.

Packing:

Start a written list of items to pack a week before you actually pack. It is so easy to forget things if you pack in a hurry. You can keep a list on your refrigerator so you can jot things down as you think of them. Some of the items on your list could include; camera, video camera, film, batteries, video tapes, notebook, tickets, reservation information, brochures, vacation agenda, deck of cards, books, magazines, pillows (if riding in the car), snacks, toys (if traveling with young children), change of clothes (a change each day plus two extras), pajamas, swim suit, socks, underwear, shoes, and toiletries. You should do the majority of washing and ironing two days before you pack. Put everything in the suitcases the day before you leave. Begin collecting things you will be taking several days before your departure. Put these items in a designated area in your house. You could use the corner in your bedroom or a spare room that is not in the way of your daily activities.

Vacation Agenda:

Whether you plan an itinerary before you leave or not, you should be flexible and wait to finalize the plans until you arrive at your destination. This gives you an opportunity to consult locals and look at brochures as a family to decide exactly what you would like to do. Write a daily schedule (which is subject to change) allowing each person to contribute their ideas. When you plan and write things down you have a better chance of doing them. It is important to have a back-up plan for your vacation schedule. When Plan A does not work be prepared to implement Plan B.

Unpacking:

When you arrive home you should be ready to resume your routine immediately. This can be difficult if things do not get unpacked quickly. Delegate jobs. Someone can unload the car, bringing everything into a central location such as the kitchen. Immediately begin unpacking the dirty laundry and start the washer. Younger children make ideal 'runners', taking things to specific rooms. Once everything is in the proper room, each family member is responsible for his own personal unpacking.

My husband and I planned a five-day get-away without children a few years ago. Our destination was Barbados. For some reason I did not follow my usual system of making lists. Everything was going according to plan. We landed on the island and checked into an expensive resort, planning to use some coupons that would allow us to stay at the hotel free. When my husband asked me for the coupons, I discovered they were not in my purse. We called my mother to help us locate the coupons at home. She sent them to us express mail. After $100 in phone calls and $50 in postage, I decided that making lists would always be a part of my future vacation planning.

Happy Vacationing!!!!

Today's Refrigerator Bulletin:
    "Vacationing is relaxing when well planned!"

Travel Agent

Q: We need some time away together as a family. We are not sure where to go or how to plan a vacation.

A: Time off from your normal routine is important. My motto is, "Work hard and play hard!" If you work many hours you need to balance this time with rest and relaxation. Begin by making provision in your household budget to pay for a family vacation. For some people you will need to save money for six months to a year. Other households may have enough cash to make immediate plans.

After reviewing each family member's schedule, select the best time for the vacation and mark that block of time on the calendar. The number of days you choose will depend on how much vacation time you have and how much money you have budgeted.

Decide where you would like to travel. We are creatures of habit and routine. Therefore we tend to repeat vacations that we have enjoyed. Go somewhere new!! If you are usually a beach hound go to the mountains. Read through travel books and magazines for ideas. Look on the Internet under travel. Rent travel videos of places to visit. Look at photo albums of friends who travel.

Consult your local travel agency for sightseeing attractions and prices. Travel agencies offer a wonderful service. They will save you time shopping for the best prices, they have access to discounts, and they have knowledge and expertise that you may lack.

You may also choose to be your own travel agent. What do you do once you have chosen your destination?

- Call and request tour information from the Bureau of Tourism or the Chamber of Commerce. They will send you information on hotels, tourist attractions, and restaurants.

- Use a local coupon book. The coupon books usually have discounts on hotels, car rentals, and amusement parks from other states.

- Call at several in the area you will be visiting. Ask about special discounts. Find out if rates includes a breakfast or any meal plan. Ask to speak with the manager. He is more likely to give you a good deal. I have saved additional money just by talking with the hotel manager.

- Call several car rental agencies to check rates. They can vary as much as sixty dollars. Make sure you get all the facts and you are comparing 'like' services. You may save money with one rental agency but rates may not include unlimited mileage. Research the facts carefully.

- Once you have booked a hotel, ask them to send you information discounts at local tourist attractions. You may even run across discounts at retail stores near your home for attractions in other towns or other states.

- Call several airlines to compare prices. Listen for radio or television ads offering special air fares. If you are not locked into a particular day there may be are discounts for weekday or weekend travel.

- Inquire of acquaintances that have visited your planned destination and get their suggestions on food, travel, accommodations and attractions. Pioneering an area is adventurous but can also create unnecessary stress.

- As you begin collecting information you will need a system to organize your materials. Keep everything pertaining to the trip in a small file box or storage container. Do not be tempted to scatter the papers on your counter where information could easily be misplaced.

Relax and enjoy the wonderful trip you have planned!

Today's Refrigerator Bulletin:
"Create the perfect vacation with organized planning!"

Family Activities

Q: My husband and I both work full-time. We have three children ranging in age from five to fifteen. It seems like we are always driving separate directions to get children to various activities. I feel we need to spend more time together as a family but I am at a loss how to accomplish this with our current schedule.

A: Plan family activities by prioritizing and scheduling time together. Each family member has his own agenda, activities, interests, and schedule. Collectively, these small streams of activity create a powerful river with a strong current. To plan family activities together, you will need to fight the current and pull everyone out of the river at once. This requires a plan, action, and willingness on the part of each family member to make the sacrifices necessary to have quality time together.

Limit the amount of extra activities in which each child participates. I know families that enroll their child in three or more after-school activities. This requires an unreasonable amount of driving at the very time you would normally prepare dinner and eat together as a family. Instead, the family dinner is bought at the drive-through window and eaten in the car or consumed in multiple shifts at home. As you plan your schedule, remember that family time is as important as the various sports activities.

Plan your schedule so you are available during your children's free time. Try to avoid planning social events with friends, a shopping spree or a late night at the office on an evening when your family is home.

Hold a family meeting to tackle the problem. Stress the importance of family time, asking each family member that is old enough to list the reasons why families should schedule time together. This list will be valuable when it is time to decide the activity schedule for the year. It is easier to compromise if everyone agrees on the basic principle.

Plan activities that are of interest to each member of the family. This is a difficult task if you have a broad age span. There are still many activities that can be enjoyed by both a pre-schooler and a teenager such as bowling (get two lanes so one can have a bumper), miniature golf, a family movie, the zoo, a museum, a botanical garden tour, an amusement park, and a picnic. Get input from each family member on what would be of interest to them and still be suitable for the entire family. Call a family meeting to discuss the activities and/or have everyone write a list. If you need ideas on available activities, get brochures from the local Chambers of Commerce or browse the bookstore for books on local sites and activities.

Schedule routine times to eat together. There are twenty-one meals in a week: Make it your collective goal to eat a specific number of them together. If it is difficult to get everyone together for dinner, arrange to eat breakfast as a family, or lunch on Saturday. Sharing meals together is fundamental for building relationships.

Establishing traditions will unite families. Plan activities that reoccur on a regular basis, perhaps yearly. Choose a favorite restaurant at which to eat together once a year. Schedule a professional family photograph each year. Take a walk in the woods, go on a picnic or take a boat ride.

Family vacations create lasting memories. Schedule a vacation at least once a year if possible. If you cannot afford the expense or time off work, schedule a one day or weekend trip to a nearby town. Send for brochures of the events in the town. Save money for a special vacation by collecting loose change in a jar. Whenever the jar is full, roll the coins and exchange them for bills. After a few years, you will discover that you have painlessly saved for a wonderful family vacation. Continue the tradition when your children are grown by including their spouses and your grandchildren on the family vacation. If you have limited financial resources, ask each family to pay for their expenses and you provide the planning.

Today's Refrigerator Bulletin:
    'Spending time with family is the bridge to happiness!'

Family Camping

Q: I would like to plan a family camping trip but I am not exactly a woodsman. Where do I start?

A: Camping can be a fun, exciting, and affordable family activity. You do not have to be an avid outdoorsman to plan a camping trip. Make your camping simple and focus on family relationships. This is an excellent way to bond as a family.

Camping offers a change from your regular routine. It provides a relaxing temporary escape from hectic schedules, phones, computers, e-mail, and video games. Replace these ordinary activities with others that would include setting up camp, food preparation, walks in the woods, fishing, boating, and swimming. One of my favorite activities while camping as a child was building stone dams in streams with my Dad. These activities can be done together as a family instead of each member following his own agenda. Include grandparents in some of your trips. We have enjoyed several three-generation camping adventures.

Camping is a way to relax "far from the madding crowds." This is one getaway that will not require standing in long lines to conquer the newest roller coaster or to gain entrance to a trendy restaurant. You are also avoiding the prices of a theme park or trendy restaurant. A walk through the woods is less costly than a walk through the mall.

This experience can also be educational. Purchase field guides and learn to identify the plants and animals indigenous to your region. Learn the constellations. The night sky in the wilderness reveals more stars than most of us could imagine. Teach your children about outdoor safety, outdoor cooking, laying a fire, and blazing a trail. Show them how to read a map and use a compass. For the really ambitious, explore the possible edible foods in the wild. Camping offers hundreds of potential adventures.

Many campgrounds provide cabins. This will add to the expense but you can enjoy some modern conveniences. If you want to rough it, you will need some basic camping supplies. If you are one of those people who must own 'state of the art' equipment, locate a good outdoor shop and start asking a lot of questions. Be prepared to spend a lot of money. Most of us can buy used items from a resale shop, surplus store, or a garage sale. You can always fall back on the outdoor store for those items you couldn't find elsewhere. Another alternative if you do not plan to make this a frequent excursion is to borrow camping gear from a friend or relative. I have included a basic supply list for your camping needs.

- Tent or camper
- Sleeping bags, blankets, cots, air mattresses, or foam pads
- Tarps/plastic sheets to cover items stored on tables or provide ground-cloths
- Umbrellas (it always rains on camping trips)
- Towels (kitchen and bath)
- Flashlights and lanterns (extra batteries)
- First aid kit (include insect repellant, sun block)
- Tools (hammer, ax, screwdriver, rope, knife, small shovel, whisk broom)
- Matches

- Guide books on plants and animals (especially poisonous snakes)
- Cooler
- Food
- Dishes and utensils for cooking and eating
- Fishing gear
- Cards, board games (playing games by fire light is a fun experience)
- Personal items (especially toilet paper)
- Portable gas stove or charcoal and lighter fluid

Organize your camping supplies in several different sized containers. Sort and group like items together for easy access. If you schedule frequent camping trips use these containers as a permanent home for camping supplies. Use containers that have tightly sealed lids. This will secure your food and supplies from raccoons and other curious critters. Raccoons are very clever and would love to share your meals.

Be prepared for the unexpected!! As a child I have fond memories of many camping experiences. We lived in the city but my Dad has always loved the outdoors so we camped a lot. On one particular weekend camping trip we had a memorable adventure. We drove to a campground a couple hours from our home and set-up camp in a beautiful valley next to a river. That night I went to sleep listening to the pitter-patter of rain on the tent. Sometime in the middle of the night my frantic parents awakened me. I was about to roll off the air mattress when I realized it was floating in a foot of water. We needed to abandon camp very quickly. The valley was steadily filling with water. We piled everything into the car and moved to higher ground where we spent the rest of the night packed like sardines. The next morning everything smelled like a wet dog. A few of the items in my suitcase bled creating a tie-dyed effect on my clothes. It was a mess but left me with an exciting memory because we pulled together as a family.

I have now chosen to share some of these special adventures with my children. Camping is not quite as fun for me now because it involves a lot of preparation and work setting up and tearing down a camp, but the memories it creates and the bonds that are forged are priceless.

Today's Refrigerator Bulletin:
"Build strong family ties thorough the adventure of camping!"

Children

Raising Children

Q: How do I balance a career, manage a home, and still spend time with my children?

A: Motherhood is a precious gift that is wrapped in joys and sorrows. The stages of childhood pass quickly so it is important to take time to enjoy each phase of our children's lives. It seems like one day we are changing diapers and in the twinkling of an eye we are buckling our seat belts tightly because our child is learning to drive.

By organizing time efficiently you can accomplish what you need to do and give your children the time they need. I am the mother of four busy children. I remember when they were younger I use to contemplate how much easier it would be to get things done when they were older. I had visions of cleaning the house without my little helpers who usually helped in reverse. My sons were less than two years apart and needed to be carefully watched. Their attempts to help me scrub the kitchen floor usually resulted in a flood of water sweeping across the linoleum because one of them would decide to tip the bucket of soapy water. Now that they are older I worry about their safety as I scrub the floor, knowing they are driving around town in their car. We tend to think the grass is greener until we cross to the other side of the fence. We need to be content and make the most of each stage in our child's life.

The 'Leave it to Beaver' days are history and most women must adapt to the demands of home and career. We live in a fast paced society that requires us to spend hours in the car. We simply can't stay at home any more. For some reason, I can't imagine June Cleaver trying to balance home and career on the same full plate. Almost as ridiculous is an image of me casually vacuuming my carpets in pearls and a dinner dress, waiting for my husband to return to his castle. Usually when I vacuum, I hope an unexpected guest does not pay me a visit because my attire would be less than presentable. But I have learned a valuable lesson from the Cleaver family; they spent quality and a significant quantity of time together.

The time you spend with each child and how you spend it will vary according to his age. Each stage of a child's life demands another level of creativity as you strive to spend time with him and still finish your tasks.

If you are one of those rare people who can do two things at once and do both with excellence, then proceed with that course of action. Include your children in work projects that are home or career oriented. For example, when children are small they can help with cleaning. Fill the window-cleaning bottle with water when the solution is gone. They will love cleaning the bathroom with their spray bottle. Make a game out of every clean-up project you do together. When they are older the same principle can apply but the projects will be different. We like to set aside one Saturday a month to work in the yard cutting grass, pulling weeds, planting, building flower boxes, and trimming. Not everyone in your household may have a 'green thumb' but each can still contribute even if simply to serve drinks and food to the yard workers. Another example: My husband and I both run our own businesses that require mass mailings. We usually rent a family movie and work together to prepare for the mailings. There are six of us so we set up an assembly line that involves folding letters, stuffing, stamping, and sealing. We take a popcorn and soda break and usually pay the children a small fee as incentive for their help. Not only are we spending time with our children but we are also teaching them organization skills. We are very busy as most households are so it is important to plan every window of time without compromising the most important thing; our relationships with our children.

Quality time with our children is important but it is still no substitute for the quantity of time we spend with them. Be creative, including them when you can and looking for ways to spend time with them. Even a catastrophe can have a silver lining. One such catastrophe happened to our oldest daughter. She had purchased a car the summer before she began college. She was attending college locally so she needed a car for her commute. Three weeks before the semester began she was in an accident that totaled her car and left her with minor injuries. The car could not be immediately replaced and she had some fear about driving so the school semester began with her Grandma, Dad, and I taking turns driving her across town. Adding this driving to my already full schedule created stress until I realized I had an hour a day of uninterrupted time to spend talking with my daughter.

Today's Refrigerator Bulletin:
"Take time from your busy schedule to enjoy each stage of your child's life!"

New Arrival

Q: We are expecting a baby. I hear stories about new mothers having no free time for months or even years. What is the best way to prepare my home and life for a new baby?

A: The arrival of a new baby is like experiencing the first day of a beautiful spring day. It brings joy, laughter, and beauty into our lives. However, if we do not properly prepare we could soon encounter stormy weather.

You will enjoy your baby more and reduce stress if you prepare your home and personal life ahead of time. Start by preparing the nursery. This includes decorating the room, and preparing the layette. This requires a variety of items but don't go out and buy everything just yet. Leave room for the possibility of a baby shower. As you get an idea what you already have and what you must purchase, use the following guidelines to help you take inventory.

The normal tendency is to buy too much so I have included the following basic items for the layette; baby bed, changing table, high chair, pumpkin seat & car seat combination, bath towels, washcloths, baby soap & shampoo, cotton balls, diapers, receiving blankets, baby quilts, sheets, bumper pad, mattress pad, waterproof pads, infant toys, sleepers, gowns, undershirts, bibs, bottles, pacifier, teething ring, training cup, baby spoon, and baby laundry soap. Additional purchases may include the following items: dresser, rocker, toy box, baby tub, walker, swing, mobile, scale, and room theme decorations. The retail stores have done a superb job of offering numerous choices in most of these categories. Unless you have an unlimited budget, you will need the discipline to select only those items you really need and limit the luxury items. If you are on a very restrictive budget buy some items at garage sales or resell shops. Another alternative is to borrow items from family and friends.

Prepare to organize your home during your nine months of pregnancy. This will allow you to spend abundant and quality time with your baby. You will need to pace yourself so you do not become exhausted. Start by reorganizing closets, drawers, and cabinets. Remove unnecessary items from your home; you will be adding another person and everything they will need. Allow for some empty space in your closets and drawers and refrain from filling them to maximum capacity. Baby items consume an enormous amount of space. If you have not had first hand experience perhaps an infant has visited your home for a couple days. You probably noticed that Mom and Dad usually made several trips to the car to carry everything in and your neat and tidy home was suddenly cluttered with baby's things.

After you have uncluttered your house begin some 'spring' cleaning projects. When the baby arrives you will not be the only master of your time so capture it while you can. If you are physically capable or you are adopting a baby you may choose to tackle these cleaning projects alone. If this is not the case hire some help or enlist your husband's assistance on evenings and weekends. These projects include the extras such as cleaning windows, the oven, and the woodwork.

You will want to limit the amount of chemicals you use in your home the first few months of your baby's life. Before delivery schedule to have your carpets cleaned. In the not-so-distant future your baby will be crawling in this territory exploring every corner. If you routinely have your house sprayed for bugs schedule a bug exterminator well in advance of the birth. You may choose to leave the house and allow your husband to handle both of these appointments.

Begin to stock up on staple grocery items several weeks before you bring the baby home. If you own a freezer you could plan some meals that could be prepared ahead of time and frozen. Lasagna and other casseroles are good full meals that can be frozen and later popped into the oven quickly for re-heating.

Avoid planning a major home project such as room additions, new flooring, or interior decorating during the first 6 months of your child's life. Plan these projects before the baby arrives. You will need time to adjust to a new household member who will grab many hours of your day.

Borrow or buy some books of interest. You can do some reading while you are feeding, rocking, and resting. You may also have some time to enjoy a favorite craft and indulge in your favorite foods. New or nursing Moms need plenty of rest, relaxation, and food. This should not include climbing ladders to wash windows.

You will need to repeat these preparations each time a new baby enters your life. If this is not your first child it is very important your other children are included in the preparations for the new baby. They will be more willing to accept their new brother or sister if they feel part of the process. Older children will be more helpful but there are jobs for the youngest members as well. They can do something as simple as place the baby's toys in the toy box.

Today's Refrigerator Bulletin:
  "Make a home plan so you can enjoy your bundle of love!"

School Preparations

Q: Summer vacation is almost over and I need to prepare my children for the school year. How can I make it simple and painless for them?

A: Changes are difficult but there are things you can do to ease the transition. Your children have been accustomed to sleeping late, enjoying pool activities, vacationing, and following an extremely flexible schedule. You certainly need to equip them with materials such as school supplies and clothes but you also need to prepare them emotionally for the change. Allow time to make the transition by beginning preparations early. Some children will be excited about the new school year while others will experience fear, dread, or disappointment. The same range of emotions is shared by all ages from kindergarten through high school. Begin taking steps in the summer to prepare your child for this sometimes difficult transition.

- Purchase school supplies early. This ensures that your child will be materially prepared and begins the process of mental preparation. School supplies are available as early as July in many retail stores. You have a month to look for bargains. Often, stores have available lists of supplies required by each of the nearby schools. You can also obtain a list from the school district's main office or your child's school. When my oldest daughter was in elementary school we did not have access to the list until the 'back to school letter' was sent out. Now I have choices. I can buy next year's supplies at the end of the current school year or get a list in mid to late summer and purchase the supplies for the fall.

- Plan a day of lunch and shopping for school clothes, shoes, a school bag (backpack), and lunch box.

- Sit down with your child and look through last school year's photos from yearbooks and your own scrapbooks or memory albums. This will remind your child of her school friends and the fun times they shared.

- Take several educational field trips during the summer to stimulate your child's mind.

- Review spelling words and math concepts before school begins. Engage your child in a summer reading program and writing activities. It is difficult to abruptly transition from watching television, playing video games, and swimming to reading, writing, and math.

- Make sure your child's alarm clock works. If not, buy a new one.

- Once you know who your child's teacher will be, ask your child to write a note introducing himself. He can tell the teacher what he did over the summer, what hobbies he enjoys, and some information about his family.

- Buy a gift for the teacher. A plant would be a good gift to take the first day. Make sure your child is included in picking out the gift.

- Plan a fun day the first Saturday after school begins. This will give your child something to look forward to in case he is dreading the beginning of school.

- Look at your own schedule and make sure you allow time to volunteer at school. Your child will be happier about school if he knows you will share his environment with him part of the time.

- Ask your child what activities he would like to do for the rest of the summer and schedule these activities.

Today's Refrigerator Bulletin:
"Bounce from summer to school with a few simple preparations!"

School Party

Q: I have been selected as room parent for my child's elementary classroom, but I am a total zero at party planning. I'm just not creative. What can I do?

A: You do not have to be creative to plan school parties. Use ideas and materials that other people have created. Purchase 'how to' books or check them out at the library. You do not need a single original idea to plan a party.

Most schools allow about one hour for the party. There are usually three parties scheduled per school year. Keep the planning simple. Have a basic plan before arranging a meeting with other parent helpers. Brainstorm ideas with them but remember you are planning a one-hour party and everyone has a busy schedule. I have been on party planning committees that met several times to plan one short party.

Your focus should be on entertaining children. Kids enjoy simple games and prizes. The same basic game can be changed according to the party theme. Take for example a younger child's game, 'Pin the Tail on the Donkey.' For Halloween, play Pin the Nose on the Jack-o-lantern, or for Christmas, Pin the Star on the Tree Top.

Do not try to do everything yourself. Delegate work and supplies. This is a classroom of children who all have parents that can contribute in some way. Full-time moms may have time to help on the day of the party or perhaps they could send baked goodies. Working moms could donate paper goods. Some schools have parent boards that contribute some money to the school parties. Apply this money to game prizes or to a guest performer such as a clown, a magician, or a storyteller.

Do a grade level party. Arrange a party with all the classes of a specific grade level. Use the combined money for a guest performer. Another option is to set-up different activities in each classroom and rotate the various classes into each of the rooms. One school year I planned a party with an international theme. Each classroom chose a country and planned a craft, game, and food associated with that country.

The easiest way to plan a party is to select a specific theme. Plan the decorations, food, games, and prizes around the theme. The holidays celebrated may depend on whether your child attends a private or public school. Most schools would celebrate in October with a Fall or Halloween party. December would be a Winter Holiday, Hanukkah, or Christmas party. February might include a Valentine's Day Party.

You may decide to make invitations by hand or use the computer. Part of the enjoyment of an event is the anticipation that it is going to happen. You can give the invitations to the teacher several days ahead of time so she can pass them out to the students.

Choose prizes at carnival supplies, mail order houses, dollar stores, or discount stores. Prizes could include candy, pencils, bookmarkers, erasers, crayons, markers, fast food coupons, and

5-cent toys (they are abandoned quickly but enjoyed for the moment).

Use paper lunch bags or zip lock bags to hold prizes. Lunch bags are available in different colors. The cheapest prize bags are the brown bags, decorated by you or the children. The children could start the party by decorating their bag with stickers, cutouts and markers. For an October party they could trace leaves on the bag or paste on a pumpkin.

If you have several parent helpers the day of the party you could plan centers with activities. Divide the children into four groups. Assign a color for each group and give each child the appropriate colored name tag so they can rotate to each center with their group. It is easier to get the attention of a group of five children than twenty.

Party ideas for elementary children for the school year (ideas may need to be modified according to the grade level):

Fall Party

Invitations:
- Write or print the party information on a pumpkin.

Refreshments:
- Popcorn, pumpkin cookies, caramel apples, orange punch or soda.

Games:
- Pumpkin relay; push the pumpkin with a broom.
- Make a giant tree on poster board. Blindfold the players and have them pin the leaves on the tree.
- Pass the pumpkin; sit in a circle and play music, passing the pumpkin. When the music stops the person with the pumpkin is out.

Crafts:

- Decorate gourds into animals using felt, plastic eyes, and yarn.

Winter Party
Invitations:
- Write or print the party information on a snowman or Christmas tree.

Refreshments:
- Decorated cookies, trail mix (different cereal, pretzels, m&ms and raisins, soda).

Games:
- Name that tune; record holiday songs and have the children guess the title.
- Bean bag toss; cut out a tree from green poster board, attach it to a box and cut out holes for the bean bags.
- Candy cane hunt; fill a box with white popcorn packaging materials and bury candy canes.
- On poster board, make a giant calendar for the month of December. Decorate with colored paper and stickers. Lay the calendar on the floor and let children take turns tossing jingle bells. You win if you hit December 24th.
- Fill a jar with candy kisses. Have each child guess how many kisses are in the jar.

Crafts:
- Photo ornament.

Valentine Party

Invitations:
- Write or print party information on a heart.

Refreshments:
- Red punch, make ice cream sundaes (vanilla ice cream , marshmallows, chocolate chips, sprinkled candy).

Group Activities:
- Decorate a box to hold valentines. Cut a hole in the top of a shoebox and decorate with stickers, dollies, cut out

hearts. Have a contest and vote for a winner on the funniest, most creative, simplest, or prettiest box. Have the children play postman and pass out valentines to each of their classmates. Send a note home ahead of time so each child would have valentines to give.

- Play valentine bingo using heart candies for markers.
- Heart puzzles. Make half the number of hearts as the number of children. Cut each one in half with a different cut. Give each child a half of a heart. Tell them to find the heart half that matches theirs.

Set up the games and crafts at centers. To establish order and bring an end to the party use the last ten minutes to read a seasonal story or play bingo. Buy paper goods to coordinate with the theme. If you do not want to follow the traditional parties, choose themes such as a carnival, a beach party, a 50's party, a backwards party, a pizza & movie video, or a party to play favorite board games.

Today's Refrigerator Bulletin:
"Simple party planning results in a smashing success!"

Babysitter's Schedule

Q: We will be leaving our children with a sitter while we go out of town. Some advice on how to make our leaving less stressful for us and the kids would be great.

A: Everything will run more smoothly if you have a written agenda and you begin your preparations early. Last minute planning is not only stressful but makes it easy to forget important matters. Put all the information in a three-ring-binder with topic dividers. On the front cover write 'Babysitter's Handbook.' Topics should include:

Important telephone numbers and addresses: Include the number of the doctor, the dentist, a close friend, at least two relatives, and a plumber. You should also leave the address and phone number where you can be reached. If you have school aged children you will need to write down the name and number of the school and carpool drivers. List the addresses and phone numbers of sporting activities or music lessons.

Schedule: Complete a written schedule for the children for each day you will be gone. Include bedtime, children's activities (with directions on where to transport them), and meal times.

Food Preparations: Stock your pantry and refrigerator with necessary food items. Make a menu and prepare some food dishes ahead of time unless your sitter is comfortable with doing all the cooking. Bake and freeze your children's favorite cookies a week or two early. Leave them on the counter with a special note the day you leave.

Children's needs: Special stuffed toy, bedtime story, favorite snack, games they like to play, fears they may have, likes, and dislikes. Explain how you would like the sitter to handle discipline.

Provide a basket for mail, and children's school papers. You will need another container for newspapers. Keep a large notepad by the phone. Write the following information across the top of the notepad; name, phone, message, date, time of call.

If the children have grandparents that are healthy and available to baby-sit they are the next best choice to Mom and Dad. If you need to hire a babysitter make sure this person has taken care of the children before you plan an out of town trip. The sitter will know some of the household routines and the children will be comfortable with someone with whom they have spent time.

Ask the sitter to spend the night the day before you leave. This will not only help the transition but the sitter can help you with packing and house preparations. If you are stressed as you leave, this could create insecurity in your children.

Offer to pay the babysitter more money to do extra household chores when she is not caring for the children. This could include laundry, light housekeeping, or changing bed linen. Make a written list for her to follow.

Make sure you financial affairs are in order before you leave. If something were to happen to you, who would take care of your children and who would handle your estate?

The person you have chosen should know how to access all necessary information and have the name and number of your lawyer.

Let your children know what you expect of them while you are gone. Do something special with them before you leave or when you return to let them know how important they are to you.

My husband and I recently left the country for a week of relaxation. We run several businesses out of our home so it is difficult for us to leave for any length of time. We needed to not only provide care for our four children, but someone needed to take care of our businesses. Our children are older so we enlisted their help to reduce Grandma's large workload. Our oldest daughter took care of the laundry, mail, and returned calls from the answering machine. Our sons unloaded the dishwasher, took out the trash, fed the dogs, and cared for the lawn. Our youngest daughter did her regular chores. The home ran smoothly during our absence because we had a written plan and left verbal instructions.

Today's Refrigerator Bulletin:
"Before you leave the nest, make sure your ducks are in a row!"

Organizing
Your Family

Family Training

Q: My family continually leaves their belongings scattered around. My husband comes in from work, dropping his papers on the counter where I need to prepare dinner. The children leave school bags on the floor and coats anywhere from the front door to the sofa. They do not put clothes or shoes where they belong. I spend too much time picking up after my family.

A: Most of us like everything neatly put away, but we live with other people who have their own standards of home organization. We need a system that everyone can agree to live by. Training the family is one effective way to keep things picked up in your house. This is not an easy task but the benefits are worth the time spent in training (Please note; it is much easier to train children than husbands). One important rule we have in our home is: "Keep things off the floor." Floor space in your home has the potential to collect clutter. It is convenient to stack things on the counter and then the floor. One of the best ways to prevent this from happening is to train your family. Daily reminders are sometimes needed as part of the training program. I compare my reminders to maintaining a car. I regularly change the oil, check the brakes, and check the air in the tires. I do not require a major engine overhaul because I have maintained my car. The same is true of my family. I routinely remind them to use it and put it away. This prevents the need for a major overhaul in my home. The reward of diligent maintenance training is an organized home.

I use a system that has brought me success in this area. I use the Shark System. I tell my family our floors are filled with sharks swimming all around. An item left on the floor is eaten and gone. Sharks are very clever and can devour items on chairs, dressers, and counters. If I find an article on the floor or counter it becomes mine for a period of time. They can earn it back by doing household chores.

Different methods are used to train husbands, older children, and younger children. The shark system is a negative and drastic approach. Positive reinforcement is also successful. For instance, the pattern of 'picking things up' is developed when your children are toddlers. They can help put toys away when you move to a new activity. Put toys away at lunch time, even if you are going to play with them after you eat. At nap time, put toys away. When your toddler wants to play with different toys, pick-up first. You can turn cleaning up into a game by clapping, singing songs, and giving lots of encouragement. Older children can earn privileges for maintaining home organization. Their reward may be the rental of a game or movie, or trip to the ice cream shop. The best way to motivate my husband is to explain that I will have more time for him if given the help I need.

Train to fail is what many women do. Their motto is: "Do as I say, not as I do!" I have seen many women frustrated over the condition of their house. They complain about their family, yet they have failed in two areas. First, they have not set an example in the area of home organization. Second, they are not consistent with their family by enforcing a standard.

Every once in a while something happens to remind me how well I have trained my family. One evening our family had gone out to dinner. When the meal was over, one of our sons, unnoticed, left the table. A few moments later he returned with his dirty dishes and, seeing our quizzical looks, replied, "I forgot I was in a restaurant. I was taking my dishes to the kitchen sink." He was embarrassed but I was proud of him. He had implemented an important principle.

Today's Refrigerator Bulletin:
"Make a list for each family member of what you expect to help you maintain a clutter free house!"

Taxi Service

Q: I am a busy Mom with many jobs. I work part-time and have three active children. I spend time driving children from one place to another. I do not feel I am using my time effectively. Any suggestions?

A: Most of us are extremely busy with jobs, running a household, driving children to activities, and running errands. We never have enough time. This seems to be the cry of our generation. One major time-consuming task is driving. You can minimize the time you spend driving by planning an efficient driving schedule. Devise a strategic plan for long and short term driving needs, a master schedule. Create a written list of errands on a weekly basis and add them to your schedule. Try to schedule appointments a month or more ahead of time. Include fixed activities like meetings, lessons, and regular appointments. Finally, add trips and social activities.

Tips for an Efficient Taxi Service:

- Schedule appointments that are geographically close for the same morning or afternoon. If your pediatrician and orthodontist are five minutes apart and a family member needs to visit both, schedule them the same afternoon. We can run an errand between appointments if time permits.

- Set-up errands according to geography. You can go to the cleaners in the same trip as the grocery store if they are close to each other. If you are meeting a friend for lunch and have an errand close to the restaurant, leave a few minutes early to handle the errand.

- Choose sporting activities closest to your house if you have a choice. For example: If your daughter wants to take dance lessons visit several studios to evaluate the facilities and teachers. If the studios are about the same in quality, choose the one closest to your home.

- Schedule errands according to traffic. Choose times with minimum amounts of traffic to do errands. If you are not stuck in traffic you will accomplish more errands in less time.

- Set up carpools with neighbors or people that live close. This is especially useful for transporting children to school and sports practices.

- Schedule one day at home if possible. Do not schedule appointments or activities on this day. This is the only way you can catch up on household chores. If you work, schedule a day off, an evening or a block of time on the weekend just to catch up on chores around the house.

- Make sure your trips are necessary. Do your children's whims require you to venture out unnecessarily? I have one child in particular that wants to buy things that are usually new to the market. When he was younger I used to drive him around from store to store when he wanted something. Now, he saves his money and calls many stores. He finds the best price and makes sure it is in stock before we drive to the store. This saves me driving time.

- Choose day care centers that are close to your home or workplace.

- When children are older you can let them bicycle to close activities. They can bicycle to the pool or a friend's house. This saves driving time in the summer months.

- Older children that have their driver's license can assist with driving. Give them gas money if they have their own car. Give them extra spending money for transporting siblings.

Today's Refrigerator Bulletin:
"Make a Taxi Service schedule!"

House Rules

Q: I am the only person in our home that puts 'things back where they belong.' How can I get other household members to help?

A: Consider the following series of events. We get in our car, turn the key until the engine roars and put the car in drive. We glance to the side and notice the speed limit sign reads 25 mph. Proceeding down the road we approach an intersection where a yellow light turns red. Our foot swiftly goes from the gas pedal to the brake. The light turns green and we proceed until we come to a stop sign. Again we put our foot on the brake until we come to a full stop. We yield to a pedestrian crossing the street before we make a right turn and finally reach our destination. We have made a decision to follow a set of rules. Rules are designed to help us and protect us, although they also inconvenience us. House rules will help us, inconvenience us, and protect us from clutter.

You can avoid picking up after your family by establishing 'house rules' and assigning chores. Rules govern behavior while chores are task related. Arrange a meeting with everyone in the household. Discuss the rules and chores then ask for additional suggestions. Hang the list in the kitchen so every household member can see it often.

House rules should be written down so everyone will understand them. When a rule becomes a house tradition or habit you do not write it on the list anymore. I have a rule not to wear shoes in our house. Everyone understands and practices this rule diligently so it is not written. Use the consequence system for breaking house rules. When a rule is broken a privilege is taken away for a period of time. If possible, the consequence should have some connection with the broken rule. For example, if someone leaves a toy in the middle of the floor it becomes yours for a period of time.

Use a reward system when your children do their chores or help in other ways. Give an allowance for chores performed. If they give you extra help you can pay them additional money, take them on a fun outing, or buy them something they have been wanting.

I am pleased when other members of my household think of something to decrease my workload. I have four children ranging from elementary school to college age. I wash and change bed linens every Monday. This is the only day my children and I do not make our beds in the morning. My three older children all enjoyed the day off until my youngest child started taking her sheets off her bed and putting them in the laundry room for me. I asked her one day why she was taking her sheets off and she replied, "I knew you took them off every Monday to wash so I decided to do it for you." What a novel idea! Angela was not very popular with her three older siblings but we have a new family tradition on Monday morning.

Another great reason to establish 'house rules' is so you will have more time to spend with your family. If everyone helps a little, then one person does not bear the burden of all the work. Your children can understand this concept. They will cooperate because they know you will have time to say yes when they want you to take them to their favorite discount store, movie rental store, park, or friend's house. Instruct your children to make sure their visiting friends understand and follow your house rules. Rules and chores teach responsibility and etiquette.

Suggestions for House Rules

- Do not wear shoes in the house
- Do not sit on the bedspreads
- No food or drinks outside the kitchen (except on special occasions when you have a family movie night and spread tablecloth on the floor)
- If you use it, you put it away
- No singing at the table
- Use kind words
- Respect the possessions of other people
- No fighting
- Put your dirty dishes in the dishwasher
- Treat others as you wish to be treated
- Put your dirty clothes in the laundry room
- Hang your bath towel up when you are finished using it
- Wear clean clothes before sitting on the furniture
- Wear a shirt and no hat at the dinner table
- Use proper table manners

House Chores (* This chore may be assigned to a specific individual and tied to their allowance or extra money earned)

- *Empty clean dishes from dishwasher
- *Feed and water pets
- *Wash and dry laundry
- *Cut the grass
- *Help with yard work
- *Set the dinner table
- Make your bed
- Put clean clothes away
- Keep your bedroom picked-up
- Wash the car

Today's Refrigerator Bulletin:
"Follow the road to an organized home by obeying the rules!"

Photo Organization

Q: I enjoy taking pictures but they need to be organized. Some of my photos are in albums but most are scattered in boxes. I can't remember dates or identities of some of the people in the pictures. Please help!

A: Lights, Camera, Action! You capture photo memories with the click of a button: vacations, Christmas, birthdays, graduations, weddings, babies, and more. You have invested money in film and development and now you need to preserve these memories so you can continue to enjoy them in the future. It is important to display your memories in an efficient, enjoyable way instead of sorting through boxes or envelopes trying to recall dates and events. I have a successful method to preserve, label, and create photo memories in a timely manner by scrapbooking.

First, schedule a time to put your photos in albums. The amount of pictures you have will determine the amount of time you spend. I work on my photos at least twice a month. I allow several hours at a time because I work with a lot of supplies and it takes time to set-up my work area. I consider working on my albums to be both a work project and a fun hobby.

Secondly, choose photo albums that are safe and will not damage your photos over time. You have spent money on film and developing: Protect your initial investment by creating a safe, enjoyable home for your photo memories. Be a wise shopper, educating yourself so you can choose the right product. Make sure the product you use is acid-free, lignin-free, and buffered. Standard photo albums contain clear plastic page covers made of PVC (polyvinyl chloride), and cardboard or paper containing acids. Over time, the polyvinyl chloride interacts with the acids, emitting chlorine gas that causes fading and discoloration to your irreplaceable photographs. Buffered pages are treated to protect your photos from acid. Another component of most paper, lignin, causes the pages on which your photos are mounted to yellow. I have seen all too many pictures ruined by the magnetic and pocket page albums.

Choose a scrapbook album that is designed for labeling directly on the page beside your photo. You will be able to label your page with important information. Make sure you label with the three basics; person, place, and date. Under some circumstances you may choose to do photo journaling, recapturing special moments. When you go on vacation, keep a daily journal of what you do. This will provide valuable information to include with your pictures after they are developed and you are ready to display them in an album. The combination of pictures and quotes from the journal will allow you to relive the events each time you view the album.

Finally, decorate your pages with photo-safe colored paper and stickers. Cutting pictures into different shapes makes the pages more interesting. Cropping pictures will make you look like a better photographer. You will be able to center your subject, remove strangers, or remove unwanted objects from your photo.

My albums look like storybooks when they are completed. Each page is my very own masterpiece. I regularly get together with friends to work on albums because it is a great time to socialize and share ideas. I know the cute little moments I freeze in time, attach to a scrapbook page, and label will be cherished memories for future generations

---

Today's Refrigerator Bulletin:
"Create photo memories in photo safe scrapbooks!"

Habits

Q: My husband and children have some bad habits that drive me crazy. The biggest problem is clutter. I hate it. They create it and don't seem to mind it, but I spend my life picking up after them. Could you offer some helpful advice?

A: A cluttered castle is often the result of bad habits and lack of discipline. Eliminating clutter will require drastic and at times painful changes in household habits. Bad habits are difficult to break but not impossible. Think about the messy habits in your household. Does someone always forget to close drawers and shut cabinets? Have you approached your bathroom vanity only to find hair and gobs of toothpaste in the sink? Does the joy of cooking drain out of you at the sight of a forgotten retainer on the kitchen counter? Is anything more frustrating than tripping over piles of dirty clothes simply because you try to put something away in your child's room? One of my greatest peeves is seeing a sink full of dirty dishes when I go to get a drink of water.

You can change habits by following four simple steps:

1. Identify the habit that is creating problems in your life.

We all have messy habits that are a source of irritation for others or ourselves. For example, a small tube of toothpaste can prove to be a major battleground in your house. Do you live in a home in which everyone squeezes the tube from the middle? Perhaps everyone squeezes it from the end. Either way is acceptable, but a problem arises when both types of toothpaste squeezers try to coexist. Individuals that squeeze from the end tend to get annoyed at the middle squeezers. End squeezers sometimes feel that they are doing all the work by making the toothpaste available to everyone else. They probably view this as an unfair situation. This proved to be a problem in our household. Although I am the primary organizer in our home, I was a middle squeezer and my husband was the frustrated end squeezer. I changed my habit to accommodate him and I am now a reformed toothpaste squeezer. I realized it required no more time to squeeze from the end and it ensured that everyone else could quickly access toothpaste, too. This is just one example of a bad habit. Engage the family in a group discussion to identify bad habits that need to be changed. Once everyone has common goals and the need for change has been publicly identified and agreed to, you are all accountable to each other. This strength in numbers will enable change.

2. Make a plan to change the habit.

It is pretty obvious that most of us resist change, yet this tendency keeps us trapped in our bad habits. After identifying bad habits, each family member must actually change their behaviors. I strongly recommend a written plan of action to help you alter a specific habit. An unwritten decision to change is easily forgotten and later abandoned altogether. Written goals lead to change. Let's stick with the example of the toothpaste. First, write down on a slip of paper, 'squeeze from the end' and attach it to the toothpaste drawer. Next, make yourself accountable to someone and ask him to regularly check your progress. This person should be a combination of drill sergeant and encouraging supporter. In order to reinforce this newly acquired habit, you will need encouragement as you progress.

3. Do it!

Do not leave room for excuses. Simply tell yourself that change is the only option.

4. Master the habit and maintain the change in your life.

Never compromise. Do not pick up the tube of toothpaste and decide just this one time you will squeeze from the middle instead of the end. Be disciplined and resist this urge. It is so easy to return to old habits because they were 'comfortable.' You need to establish a new regimen, creating a new 'comfort zone.'

Today's Refrigerator Bulletin:
"Habits change when you identify, write a plan and do it!"

Holidays

WE LOVE YOU,
DAD

Father's Day

Q: I want to do something unique to honor my Dad on Father's Day. I would like to buy him something other than a necktie.

A: Seize every opportunity to honor the special people in your life. Don't let Father's Day pass you by without truly celebrating your dad. If your own father is no longer living or you are not in relationship with him, adopt a dad. Father's Day is a time to express your love in words and action. You can plan an elaborate celebration or something simple. He will be easy to please because fathers generally have few expectations about being celebrated and honored. Surprise him and make it a special day. You can still celebrate in a big way with minimum cost. Here are several gift and activity suggestions:

- Design your own card on the computer or make one from construction paper. Your own handwritten words from the heart will mean more to him than the best factory card ever produced.

- Wrap his gift in newspaper or a brown grocery bag. You can decorate the bag with clippings from the sports page or a self-portrait. Besides demonstrating what an economical, creative person you are, you can remind him of the joy of receiving simple gifts from a child.

- Buy him a gift to support his favorite hobby.

- Ask him to make you a list of what he would like. Tell him the list need not be limited to store bought items.

- Tell him you would like to spend the day with him doing whatever he would enjoy most.

- It is said, "A way to a man's heart is through his stomach." Create a dinner menu with several choices of appetizers, a main course, salads, desserts, and drinks. Give him the menu several days ahead of time and take his order. On Father's Day present him with his special dinner.

- While he is away from his office decorate it with streamers, balloons, and signs. They could say: 'Happy Father's Day to the Best Dad in the World!' 'I'm glad to be your kid!' 'You will always be number one with me!' 'I love you more than words express!'

- Shopping is not usually the way most men spend their free, relaxing time. Therefore many men do not buy clothing for themselves, especially if there is a woman in their life to do it for them. Do not hesitate to buy the traditional gifts that include ties, shirts, socks, and handkerchiefs.

- If your dad enjoys sports and outdoor activities consider one of the following; tickets to a sporting event, a fishing license, golf lessons, or coupons for a tee time.

- Some Dads may enjoy getting gag gifts. If your Dad has expressed a desire for a red sports car buy him a toy car similar to the one he would like to own.

- Buy a gift that he could use with his business. One of my husband's businesses is ownership in a painting company. I gave him a paintbrush and I wrote a personal message and included the date and occasion. Anything you can do to personalize a gift will give it special meaning.

- Pull together a 'House Treasure Hunt' with a prize at the end of the clues. Make your clues into rhymes. Each clue will bring him to a new location in the house until he eventually wins his gift. Some rhymes could be: 'In the room you sleep, look under the heap!' You're doing fine, it is time to dine!' 'Look on the wall down the long dark hall!' 'You watch me, but you I can't see!'

- Play a television game show but create some of your own rules. We once combined 'The Price is Right' with 'Let's make a Deal!' We bought several gifts big and small such as a candy bar, a can of mixed nuts, a key chain, a shirt, and a tie. He had to guess the price of several of the items. If he guessed within a specified amount he won the item. Finally he had an opportunity to go for the grand prize behind one of three doors. Door one had nothing behind it. Door two had an inexpensive item. Door three had a new shirt. Of course, our plan was to give him all the gifts when the game was over. He had a lot of fun and we all shared some good laughs and memories.

Today's Refrigerator Bulletin:
"I love you is the best gift of all!"

Mother's Day

Q: I have a great mom. I need some ideas on how to make Mother's Day really special for her.

A: In 1914, in the midst of industrial revolution and a world 'ruled' by the likes of the Rockefellers, the Carnegies, and the Morgans, this nation decided that the second Sunday of May should be set aside to honor mothers. Mother's Day is still a traditional holiday in most American homes. Despite this appropriate gesture, Mother's Day does not have to be confined to one day a year. The following thoughts include ways to bless your mother on Mother's Day and throughout the entire year. The relationship with one's mother is special and should be enjoyed. If you have lost your mother due to death or relationship difficulties, adopt a mother.

Whether you are a mother yourself or you have a mother and mother-in-law to honor on this designated day, I have listed ways you can honor your mother on Mother's Day and any day throughout the year. We shouldn't get hung up on the day since many of our mothers live too far away to be with us on the second Sunday in May. Here are some suggestions for <u>Honoring Mom:</u>

- Share her favorite hobby. If she is a member of a quilting group, see if you can join her on the day she quilts. This will give you an opportunity to meet her friends and watch her quilt.

- Follow an established tradition such as sending her flowers and candy.

- Prepare a special dinner at your house or hers.

- Offer to repair something in her home.

- Put pictures from the past in photo albums. Have her tell stories about her childhood and yours. Record the memories in the albums so you can share them with your children.

- Present her with a picture of your family in a decorative frame.

- Go to a day spa together.

- Spend a day of shopping and have lunch together.

- Spend a day together at a beauty shop indulging in a new hairstyle and a manicure.

- Go to the art museum, a monument, stroll along the waterfront, or go to the park.

- Plant flowers in her yard and pull some unwanted weeds.

- Send her a singing telegram expressing how grateful you are to have her for a mom.

- Make a gift and card for her.

- Do her grocery shopping and laundry for a week.

- Hire a cleaning service for her home.

- Husbands, become a 'Mom' for the day. Release your wife to spend the day doing her favorite things.

- Buy or make a coupon book of promised services that could include unloading the dishwasher, washing the car, folding the laundry, and providing back rubs.

- The restaurants are crowded on Mother's Day and the waiting time for seating is usually quite long. I established my own tradition: I prepare a simple meal at home and invite my Mother and Mother-in-law. I would rather cook and enjoy the intimacy of family than celebrate in a crowded room with strangers.

- I have methodically woven traditions into our family. Traditions connect us as a family in a unique way. My children established a Mother's Day tradition of serving me breakfast in bed, followed by gift opening and photo shots of Mom's first waking hour. After several years of looking at myself memorialized on film with no make-up and wild hair I suggested a change in the tradition. We now have breakfast at the table after everyone is dressed for the day. I much prefer to eat breakfast with my family than by myself in a bed full of crumbs anyway.

My children voted and decided there should be a 'Children's Day.' I had to inform them everyday was children's day.

Today's Refrigerator Bulletin:
"Do not delay: Give your Mom a hug today!"

Christmas Wrapping

Q: I never enjoy the month of December because of all the preparations and expenses. I spend late nights wrapping presents. Sometimes I have to unwrap a gift because I forget to whom it should go. How can I make this a 'holiday season' instead of drudgery?

A: Summer is over, autumn begins and the holidays are quickly approaching. You need to buy Christmas gifts and have your purchases wrapped before December 25th. All this work can steal the fun away from the holidays. Set a goal to complete Christmas gift preparations by the first week of December. This is attainable and it allows you to spend the remainder of the month enjoying holiday activities. There are three guidelines to follow when you purchase and wrap Christmas gifts. This process must be efficient, economical, and enjoyable.

Efficient:
Start shopping for Christmas in August. You will have the opportunity to take advantage of sales. Try to complete most of your shopping by Thanksgiving. You will need to arrange an area to store these gifts. I have several large shelves in my basement on which to store my gifts. Use a computer or hand written list to keep track of the people you shop for and the gifts bought. Type each person's name and list the gifts for each

289

individual. This list is important to use when you are shopping and wrapping. Take the list to the store when you Christmas shop and write down what you have purchased next to the person's name. Once the gift is wrapped, circle the individual's name and gift on the shopping list. This will help you keep track of the purchased and wrapped gifts. Begin wrapping in November. Create a wrapping center somewhere in you home. I use my basement. This allows time for short or long wrapping sessions, because supplies are always ready. Arrange three tables in a "U" shape with a chair in the middle. One table is empty for wrapping. Another table is used to rotate wrapped and unwrapped presents. The last table has supplies separated into categories. Wrapping materials are divided into containers; paper, tissue, ribbon, bows, tags, tape, scissors, pen, and a shopping list. Gifts are wrapped early so you have several weeks to enjoy the beautifully decorated gifts.

Economical:

Wrapping materials are expensive, especially when you consider that most of it ends up in the trash in a matter of minutes. You need to be efficient and thrifty with wrapping. Buy your supplies on sale and store them yearly. After Christmas, everything is drastically discounted. This is a good time to stock up. Look for other bargains throughout the year. For instance, green, red, gold, and silver ribbon/tissue can be purchased year round. Discounted paper supplies can be found on a regular basis. Handmade supplies are cheaper. Decorate paper bags with stickers and stencils. Cards can also be made. You can buy card stock paper with envelopes in large quantities at a local printer. Create your own cards using photos, stickers, colored pens, and cutouts from colored paper. Not only is the time spent on these cards worth the savings but the personal touch carries more meaning.

Enjoyable:

You will want to enjoy the month of December and not feel the pressure of holiday preparations. If your shopping, wrapping, and sending of cards and gifts are done by the first of December you can devote the rest of the month to baking, parties, and sight-seeing with guests from out of town.

Each year watch the hustle, bustle, and rush of everyone at Christmas and be thankful for your system. 'IT WORKS!'

Today's Refrigerator Bulletin:
"Wrapping should be efficient, economical, and enjoyable!"

Holiday Frenzy

Q: Holiday preparations usually stress me out. I spend so much time on preparations I do not enjoy the social events. I want to look forward to the holidays and not dread the months of November and December.

A: Scheduling time for holiday preparations is an awesome task. It is difficult because people naturally tend to fill all available space and time. Trying to add additional tasks and activities will naturally create stress. When you schedule each minute of a twenty-four hour day it is easy to panic in mid-November. Enjoy the holiday season by planning ahead and keeping things simple.

Simple tips to smoothly sail through the holiday season:

- Do not plan and cook the Thanksgiving meal by yourself. Coordinate a potluck Thanksgiving dinner and ask everyone to bring her favorite dish to share. Create this new tradition so you can spend more time with your guests instead of exhausted in the kitchen.

- Hire a neighborhood child to help you bake cookies and wrap gifts.

- Make a list ahead of time of the names of people for whom you want to purchase a gift. Do not wait until the holiday season has already begun. Look through catalogs for ideas and write the ideas down as they come to you. This will enable you to shop with focus.

- Shop during off-peak times at the mall to avoid crowds and reduce time waiting in lines. Some of the best shopping times include weekdays during the day (avoid noon), around the evening mealtime, or late at night. If you must shop on weekends, try to go very early or very late in the day.

- Order gifts from the catalog of a reputable company with quality merchandise. Some catalog companies offer unique gifts that cannot be purchased anywhere else.

- Gifts that are easy to acquire and are greatly appreciated include coupons to events or stores, baskets filled with food items, and gifts such as note cards that are personalized with names or initials.

- Use a bread maker to make homemade breads as gifts.

- Make baked goods ahead of time and freeze them.

- Decorate with half of your usual holiday decor. Your house can still look festive with less effort. Give some of the extra items to a charitable organization.

- Wrap gifts immediately after you have bought them. Be sure to label the box with the recipient's name and keep a separate list of the contents of each box.

- Delete some activities from your schedule during the holiday season. Limit your volunteer work and extra household projects in November and December.

- Establish family traditions such as dinner at a new restaurant during the month of December.

- Draw names for gift exchanges early.

- Address cards before the holiday season begins.

- Trade services with a friend. If you have a knack for baking and a friend has a good eye for decorating, bake holiday treats for her and let her decorate your home.

- Start all the preparations early so you can enjoy social events. You do not want to sit at a party thinking about all the gifts that need to be wrapped.

- Most importantly, relax and enjoy the holiday season with family and friends.

Today's Refrigerator Bulletin:
"Avoid holiday madness by simplifying holiday preparations!"

Rotating Decorations

Q: I enjoy celebrating the holidays. How can I decorate my house for each holiday with minimum effort and money?

- A: New Year's, Valentine's Day, St. Patrick's Day, Easter, 4th of July, Halloween, Thanksgiving, Hanukkah, and Christmas. Decorations are part of the celebration of these holidays. Each year it is a challenge to know how much time and money to devote to each holiday. Use some of the following suggestions, and be selective about holidays for which to decorate your home.

- Use handmade items when possible. If you buy decorations, do so a day or two after the holiday. You will often enjoy discounts of 50% or more.

- As you find new decorations be willing get rid of others. Give the outgoing items to a friend (a friend may have commented on how much she likes a decoration), sell at a garage sale, or give to a charity.

- Decorate your house anytime from two weeks to one month before the day of the holiday, allowing time to enjoy the festive mood created. Return decorations to their storage box the day after the holiday.

- Decorate walls, shelves, counters, and tables.

- Choose the easiest way to decorate a room. A year-round item is exchanged for a holiday decoration. The process is simple. Remove the year-round decoration and replace it with the holiday decoration. Temporarily store the year-round decoration in the holiday storage box.

- Here are some examples of decorations you could use; kitchen towels, pot holders, fingertip towels, wall plaques, music boxes, small quilts, candles, pillows, dishes, glasses, serving platters, and bowls.

- Limit your decorating to a few rooms such as the living room, dining room, hall bath, family room, and kitchen.

- You can decorate the outside of your home with a doormat, wreath, flag, and mailbox arrangement for each holiday.

- Store your decorations in clear plastic containers in your basement or attic. Separate on shelves by holiday and label each container. Exchange year-round decorations for the holiday decor, putting them in the plastic containers.

I can decorate for some holidays such as Easter and Thanksgiving in about an hour. Christmas decorations take me about eight hours. I break-up my Christmas decorating into several sessions:

1. I exchange my china and stemware in the dining room hutch with my Christmas dishes and glasses.

2. A large percentage of wall decorations are removed and replaced with wreaths, quilts, flowers, etc. Christmas towels are hung in the kitchen and bathroom.
3. Outside lights are hung from trees, bushes, and the house. The mailbox is decorated with greenery. A lighted wreath is hung by the door. A holiday doormat is placed on the porch. Finally the flag is hung from the flag pole.
4. Putting up the Christmas tree is an event for the entire family. It is a tradition for the six of us to decorate the tree together. Each of our four children have his/her own box of ornaments labeled with his/her name. We give each child a new ornament in December. As each leaves home he will have enough ornaments for his first tree. Everyone helps put the tree together, untangle the lights, test the lights, and hang the ornaments. The younger children take turns each year putting on the tree topper. We play Christmas music, drink hot chocolate, and eat cookies. We capture these moments with photos and video.

My goal is to complete my Christmas preparations by the first week of December.

Today's Refrigerator Bulletin:
"Keep your decorations simple, affordable, and enjoyable!"

Shopping

<u>Shopping</u>

Q: I enjoy shopping. My husband says, "Shop only for what you need spending the least amount of money possible. A sale is not a bargain, just extra money spent." How do I convince him I need and want to shop?

A: Most women like to shop because it fulfills social and emotional needs. Meeting a friend for lunch and shopping is pleasurable. It is a great opportunity to spend time with one friend or a group. Women gain self-worth from shopping. Buying new clothes improves our appearance and self-image. Accomplishing goals for the home is another benefit of shopping. We create a mental list of treasures that would enhance the quality of life in our home. As we shop, we suddenly see one of the treasures on a list; a picture that is just perfect for an odd wall, a bowl that is just the right size for those big salads I like to make, etc. We experience satisfaction knowing we have fulfilled a need for our home or family. It is even more satisfying when we find a bargain in the process. Men need to understand that, to women, shopping is more than a mechanical exchange of money for merchandise.

There are different types of shoppers. Many women fall into all of these categories depending on the circumstances. Some of these categories are defined below:

Practical Shopper
Ms. Practical is on a mission. She keeps a list of her shopping needs. She shops according to needs, not pleasure. She purchases functional items. She shops sensibly making sure each item is necessary for the household. She carefully spends according to the household budget.

Bargain Shopper
Ms. Bargain heads straight for the discounted items. She looks for the "best" deal. Stocking up on sale items is her plan. She shops for needed items but in addition buys for fun because, after all, "It's on sale!"

Browse Shopper
Ms. Browse has time to stroll leisurely through the store. She finds pleasure in "just looking." She occasionally buys but prefers to slowly investigate what is available.

Impulsive Shopper
Ms. Impulsive enters the shopping mall with charge cards ready. If she likes it, she buys it! The family budget has little impact on her shopping excursion. She accumulates many unused items because she buys them quickly and without a thought for how she will use them.

Your husband should understand that you may need to do each of the above from time to time. That is because our emotional needs, available money, available time, or other circumstances influence the kind of shopping we do. For example, I am usually a practical and/or bargain shopper. When I shop with friends I browse. When we are on vacation I look for a bargain but also shop impulsively. I especially enjoy shopping in Mexico because they negotiate prices. I shop impulsively because it may be my only chance to buy a particular item.

Give your husband the following explanation: Shopping is like golf, football, or baseball. It fulfills an emotional need. Search for a sale on his favorite ice cream, chocolate candy, or a tool he wants. Present it with a hug and say, "Honey, I chose this especially for you and it was on sale." He may feel the money spent was well worth it.

Today's Refrigerator Bulletin:
"Shop for pleasure and purpose!"

Purse Organization

Q: How do I shop to find a purse to fit my needs?

A: A purse should be serviceable and efficient, not functioning as a 'clutter bin.' It is important that you purchase the kind of purse that will best suit your needs. Purses not only come in various sizes, shapes and colors, they also function differently. Some have zippers while others have snaps, buttons, velcro, a drawstring, or an open compartment. Purses also are constructed differently. They have numerous compartments or just one large compartment. Purses are important to women and very personal. The items in a woman's purse contribute to her identity and satisfy her needs. Think twice about buying a purse for a gift unless you know the individual very well.

Purses have many different uses. For special occasions, keep smaller purses in several different colors that match dress shoes. These purses work for short periods of time because they do not usually have the space to hold everything a women needs on a daily basis. Some purses can be carried on the shoulder and some on the arm. A shoulder bag allows your hands to be free for carrying other items. Wearing a purse around your waist is great for long days at an amusement park, the zoo, or a museum. You may want to consider seasonal purses. A good summer purse could be lighter in color, made out of straw or constructed with a printed fabric. A winter purse would be darker in color and made of leather or vinyl fabric. A good system to keep an organized purse is to clean it out weekly and when you change to another purse.

Spend time shopping before you purchase a purse. It is important to purchase a purse in which it is easy to find items and easy to keep organized. I found out the hard way that I do not like purses that have numerous compartments. Because I am an organized person I assumed I would like a purse with many compartments so I could sort and put like items together. It works in my closets and with my dresser drawers but not with my purse. I purchased this kind of purse and discovered that every time I needed to locate my keys quickly I had to unzip three zippers before I could locate them. I like a purse with one big zipper that I can open and see all the contents at once. I like one extra small compartment where I keep extra keys that are not on my key chain. I separate the items in my purse by purchasing organizers such as a make-up bag, coupon sorter, wallet, envelope for receipts, and an envelope for other papers that require my action when I am doing errands. This envelope would contain documents for car inspection, coupon payment book for the orthodontist, shopping list, etc.

It is hard for me to purchase a purse on the spur of the moment. I had to make an exception, however, when we were on a family vacation visiting some relatives in a warmer part of the country. We were staying at their home enjoying their superb hospitality. Our personal items, including my purse were in the closet of the guest room. One day I went to the closet to get my purse as we prepared for an outing. I lifted it from the floor and noticed rapidly moving black specks. Upon further inspection I discovered ants crawling in & out and up & down my purse. I quickly carried my purse downstairs and out the door, calling for help as I went. We emptied the contents, which were covered with masses of ants, and brushed off each item.

We tried removing them from inside the purse but were not successful because they kept reappearing. The ants had found their way inside the purse lining so we made a small cut to try to get them out. The purse was destroyed in the process and I had to go emergency purse shopping. I purchased a purse but used it for only a short period of time because it did not suit my needs. I needed more time for such an important purchase.

Today's Refrigerator Bulletin:
   "Brown, white, large, small, zipper, snap, choose the purse that fits you best!"

Household Purchases

Q: Our house is cluttered with lots of things. Our closets are packed beyond capacity. I do not know where to put new things when I return from shopping.

A: In order to manage a household you will constantly be making purchases. If you have an active buying system, it is important to have a corresponding purging system. If you keep filling space you will eventually run out of space. Make it a rule to keep rooms, closets, drawers, and cabinets at eighty percent capacity or less. By doing so you should never face the dilemma of crammed rooms and stuffed closets.

Large items take up lots of space. Before you buy a large item do a sketch of the room layout so you will know where to place your new purchase. Visualize what it will look like and make sure it will fit in your room. If the item replaces a current item in your home then remove the old one first. My parents bought us a new ping pong table. I did not arrange for delivery until I found a home for our old ping pong table. Even though we had space in our basement for both tables, I live by the rule to remove the old before bringing in the new.

If you are adding an item to your room make sure it does not block traffic flow. Limit the number of furniture pieces in each

311

room so you will be able to move unimpeded from one room to another. Constantly moving and maintaining items consumes enormous amounts of time.

Store knick-knacks and other collectibles items in a cabinet with shelves and glass doors. Dusting will be kept to a minimum.

Before you go on a wardrobe shopping spree purge your closet of clothing you do not wear. Before you go to the grocery store make sure there is room in your pantry and refrigerator for the new food items.

Do not buy on a whim if it will jeopardize your family budget or create clutter in your house. The quality of what you buy should be determined by how long you want to keep the item. Is the item a lifetime purchase or something you just need for a period of time? Items you plan on keeping for a lifetime should be made of better quality materials.

Familiarize yourself with prices and look for sales. If you are patient most items will eventually go on sale. Ask the retail store when they expect the item to go on sale. Plan ahead and save money.

Save receipts on each item you buy. If it plugs in or runs on batteries it usually has a one year warranty. Keep and store the receipt inside the original box for a year. For large items you will need to keep the receipts in a folder labeled 'home receipts.'

Today's Refrigerator Bulletin:
   "Shop smart to save time and money!"

Economical Grocery Shopping

Q: Buying groceries and eating out are expensive. How can I spend less money without sacrificing nutrition in my meals?

A: You may be able to spend significantly less money on groceries if you change the way you currently shop. It will require more of your time because you will have to research food prices and drive to several stores.

To maximize your dollar you will need to shop at more than one of the grocery stores in your area. Read the sales inserts in your free local paper or mail advertisements. Another option is to review the advertisement at the store. Stores have discounts on specific products each week. Make sure you have researched prices of items most commonly used by your household. Stock up on these items when they are on sale. You may need to keep a written list to stay abreast of price changes in each store. Assume nothing about prices without the proper research. I assumed one of my local discount grocers would charge less for milk than a full service grocer. The cost at the discount store was more. Always have a written list of what you need to buy. As you shop at several stores do not be tempted to buy items that are not on your list. You will spend more money on groceries.

Use coupons from the stores, newspapers, magazines, and the mail. Many people do not take the time to use coupons and end up throwing them away. Ask friends and relatives to give you the coupons they will not be using. Find out when a store is having a double or triple coupon day. Coupons are usually for name brand items. Sometimes a generic brand of the same product has equal quality and is less expensive than the brand name product, even with the coupon.

You will pay extra for luxury and convenience. You must decide what is worth more to you. Discount grocery stores may have lower prices but they do not pamper you by bagging your groceries or offering curb service. A floral service or video rentals may not be available. Items on the shelves are stocked in boxes instead of pleasant displays. The stores may not be spotlessly clean. They may charge a rental fee to use a shopping cart and charge you for the bags. You still need to research prices and quality. Do not assume prices are lower just because the conditions are not as nice.

It takes time to shop at several grocery stores. Schedule your time in an efficient way. You may choose to shop at all the local stores in one day or you may stop at various stores throughout the week while en route to other errands. In the warmer months, carry a cooler in which to store perishable items to prevent spoilage while you make other stops.

Buy fresh fruits and vegetables at a local produce store or stand if available in your area. Products will be fresh and often less expensive. Be sure to compare prices to those in the grocery stores.

Avoid frozen fast food items. They are expensive and not as nutritious. However, if you and your spouse both work you may need some quick meals, so buy frozen foods when they are on sale. Another alternative to frozen fast foods is an evening meal prepared that morning. If you work late or need to transport children to afternoon sports events, put a quick meal in the crock pot before work instead of resorting to fast foods.

Do not shop according to your taste buds but purchase items that are on sale. If there is a tremendous deal on apples but your family's first choice is oranges and their second choice is apples, then buy the apples. Oranges will be on special another week.

The most expensive way to feed your household is to eat out. Restaurants or fast food establishments will quickly consume your food budget. Instead, arrange a special night once a month to eat out as family and stick to your plan.

If time is a more precious commodity to you than money, you will want to modify this shopping plan. You may think it worthwhile to shop at only one or two stores. Even so, take the time to comparison shop for several weeks so that you shop at the stores that consistently give the best deals. In any case, adapt your shopping to the priorities in your particular household.

Although technically they are not groceries, purchasing toiletry items can be particularly tricky. Often, the prices on such items at grocery stores are inflated. They take advantage of the public's appetite for convenience. Usually, a discount department store is more economical. And again, do your homework. Some so-called discount drug and department stores are no less expensive than the grocery stores. Also keep in mind that these stores run sales and specials as well.

Today's Refrigerator Bulletin:
"The money you save on food will be spent on time!"

Maintaining
Relationships

Correspondence

Q: How do I sustain and build relationships with people and still keep up with life's numerous commitments?

A: The best way to build strong relationships is to spend time interacting with the people you care about on a regular basis. The strength of a relationship is in the foundation you build. The best building blocks are the times you spend together and the exchange of encouraging words along with listening ears. Building this kind of time into a busy schedule can be difficult, so start with some strategic planning and follow through! How often have you promised to write a letter or call someone but it never quite happens. Nurturing a relationship requires planning and effort.

Schedule time to write letters or notes to the important people in your life. Sometimes, these will be informative but more often, they simply send the message that you care about the recipient and are thinking about them. If you have difficulty expressing yourself in writing, buy some books with cute sayings or quotes that will add flavor to your notes. Take a minute out while shopping to read greeting cards to give you great ideas and stimulate your creativity. Write quick notes to the people that you see on a regular basis. You want to bring a smile to that special person's face as they discover and read your note. I have written a funny or romantic message on a post-it-note to my husband and put it on the steering wheel of his car. I have also used a bar of soap to write him a message on the shower stall.

Words are powerful and can strengthen a relationship. Over the years my husband and I have written messages and put them in our children's lunch boxes from time to time. I usually write a sweet message like, "Have a wonderful day honey, and I will see you when you get home from school!" The contents of my husband's messages are typically funny. He will put extra cookies in the lunch box and enclose a note that says, "I bet you can't eat all these chocolate chip cookies!"

Modern technology has given us more options than ever for building long distance relationships. You can type letters on the computer to send via fax or e-mail. Long distance rates are becoming less expensive every day, and some long distance calls become local with certain wireless plans. But don't let today's technology keep you from sending a hand written letter. Computers are fast, efficient, and have great spell checkers, but they are still no substitute for your unique handwriting.

Schedule a block of time once or twice a month for correspondence. Write a reminder on your calendar and keep the most recent letter from each correspondent in an accessible place so you can refer to it as you write. Use this time for writing thank you notes, sending friendship cards, filling out invitations, and, writing long distance letters. Prepare birthday and anniversary cards ahead of time. Keep them in storage container and remember to mail them at the appropriate time in the month. Take time to send baby congratulations and get well cards on the spur of the moment.

Keep an abundant supply of stationary, note cards, and greeting cards. You will not only have them available when you need them but by planning you can take advantage of sales. Paper products are rather expensive disposable items so you will want to shop store sales or order through mail catalogs.

Preparing holiday cards can be either a chore or pleasant experience. By planning, you can avoid the frustration of last minute preparations. I enjoy addressing and writing notes in my Christmas cards because I create a festive atmosphere. I sip hot chocolate and eat cookies while I watch a holiday movie or listen to Christmas music. I begin the process in November to avoid suffering from the 'holiday rush syndrome.'

Do not limit your correspondence to necessary communications, such as birthday congratulations or invitations. Send a note or make a phone call just to say, "I was thinking about you and I appreciate you."

Today's Refrigerator Bulletin:
    "Written and spoken words build strong relationships!"

Gift Giving

Q: I desperately need birthday and holiday gift ideas. Some people on my shopping list are difficult to buy for and I am afraid I'll buy something I have already given them. Save me from this embarrassment.

A: It is a continual challenge to shop for the 'special' people in your life. Each time, you have to consider such issues as, "Will he like it?", "Does he have one already?", "Is it within my budget?"

Follow a few simple rules in gift giving:

- Surprise the person with a gift or ask him for a list of items that would interest him.

- Before choosing a gift for someone, observe her wants and needs. Visit her home, watch what she wears, and what she does. Ask the expertise of someone who knows her better than you do.

- Plan ahead so you can take advantage of store sales and you will have time to shop for the perfect gift.

- Keep your receipt in an accessible location in case you need to make an exchange or return a gift.

- Make a list of the people you shop for and the gifts you give them. Keep this list for several years so you can use it as a reference to avoid duplicating the gift several years in a row.

- Walk through a mall or discount store. You will accumulate ideas just by walking from one aisle to the next. It is also a great way to scout sales because many items are discounted 50%-75%.

- Some people have a hobby such as fishing, golfing, or sewing. Others are collectors of items such as sports cards, thimbles, or plates. Make a purchase that would contribute to their collection or area of interest.

Listed below are basic and creative gift ideas:

Man (Dad): Tie, shirt, socks, sports tickets, pen set, desk organizer, cologne, sports cap, belt, tools, watch.

Woman (Mom): Perfume, blouse, jewelry, scarf, inspirational quotes, a book about Moms, flowers, film, linens, house ware products, monogram sweatshirt, coupons to help around the house, perfumed soap, lotion, bath splash.

Baby/Toddler: Stuffed animal, musical toy, sand toy, pull toy, pool toy, building blocks, clothing, hat, book.

Teenager: CD, movie tickets, head phones, fad t-shirt, mall gift certificate, telephone card, phone, movie video, backpack.

Boys (Brother): Car, truck, computer game, video game, board game, sports cards, model, sports t shirt or sweatshirt, book.

Girl (Sister): Doll, baby doll, doll or baby accessories, jewelry, beanie baby, hair accessories, book, clothing, play make-up, stuffed toy, game.

Grandparent: Plant, handkerchief, stationery, framed photo, photo album, tote bag, stamps, wrapping supplies, craft kit, box of all occasion cards, case for reading glasses.

Friend: Lunch coupon, friendship plaque, friendship book, hand-made item, picture frame.

Teacher: Book store gift certificate, decorative note pad, pens, pencils, assortment of stickers or awards.

Boss/Secretary: Pencil organizer, desk organizer, floppy disk organizer, plant, day off coupon, dinner coupon, box of candy, fruit basket.

Pet: Chewing bone, pet toy, food or water dish, decorative collar, grooming coupon.

Design a card to coordinate with the gift you buy. For your convenience some suggestions are listed below:

Watch   'Every moment with you is a treasure!'
Framed picture   'An important memory in time!'
Jewelry with stones 'You are a precious gem!'
Stuffed toy   'Sweet dreams!'
Sports tickets   'You are always a winner with me!'
Plant   'You grow sweeter each year!'

Today's Refrigerator Bulletin:
  "Bought, wrapped, and given in love!"

Work Projects

Q: We both work, yet our house is begging for some attention. How do we work home repair/improvement projects into our hectic schedule and tight budget?

A: There is no end to the projects a homeowner must tackle. Just as you finish wallpapering the hall bathroom and while you are cleaning up you notice the kitchen wall needs a touch up paint job because of the grease splattered from last nights' dinner. You go down-stairs to look for the can of paint and lose your balance because the handrail has become detached from the stairwell wall. Frustrated with this series of events, you remember your 'honey do list.' This includes painting the exterior of the house, building a flower box under the bay window, and staining the baseboards in your daughter's room. You are on a 'Merry-go-round' of work projects. You need a workable system if you are going complete them.

Get together with a circle of your close friends to list all the major projects each household must complete. Then, pool your efforts. Schedule a series of workdays. On each workday, everyone will converge on one house and tackle a project. The next work day, you will go to a different house and a different project. There are several advantages to this plan:

- **Each person will contribute his area of expertise**. Skills and experience level will vary greatly. Find something that each person can do well and assign tasks. One will have a needed tool or piece of equipment, another may be a highly skilled craftsman, while another makes an ideal organizer. Everyone will have an important job, from the supervisor to the sandwich maker.

- **You will save money**. It is a major expense to hire companies or individuals to do repair work in your home.

- **You can combine work and play**. As you complete projects, you can enjoy fellowship with people you care about. When you visit each other's homes in the future you will share a sense of pride knowing you have contributed to the beauty and functionality of that home.

This system is not limited to repair work: You can do the same thing with cleaning and organizing. There are skills involved in keeping a clean, clutter free home. These skills can be shared and put into action as you help each other. Gather a group of friends and plan a day to work in one home. The hostess for the day should prepare a simple meal such as dollar rolls with cheese and lunch meat, chips, fruit, brownies, and drinks. She should also have a plan for a home project and provide the necessary supplies. The projects could include washing all the windows, organizing a closet, cleaning out a basement, or pricing items for a garage sale. An all-day task for one person is completed in a few hours by the group.

Once your group is established, you can be available to help each other when the need arises. A very close friend of ours called one day and asked if we had anyone available to help him pull staples out of his hardwood floors. Fleas had recently invaded his carpet and because the carpet was old he decided to take this opportunity to remove it. This was not a planned project yet he needed help removing the staples and tack boards. My husband and I were glad to rearrange our schedule to spend time helping. The job was completed in a third of the time and we enjoyed the time with our friend.

Today's Refrigerator Bulletin:
   'A huge project can be simplified with the help of friends'

Date Night

Q: Our life is so busy with work, children's activities, and time spent with extended family that my husband and I feel we do not spend enough time with each other. Our conversations are limited to coordinating our schedules. How do we keep our relationship fresh and alive?

A: People tend to fill all space and time in their lives. You should carefully choose how you fill your time. A good way to keep your marriage alive and thriving is to have a weekly date night. Choose a night that is agreeable for both of you. Protect your date night by not scheduling other activities on that night. If you have young children, arrange for a regular babysitter and line up a back-up babysitter just in case. Make sure date night does not become a boring routine. Keep it fresh by planning ahead sometimes and other times doing something spontaneous.

The benefits of a weekly date night are many:

- Enhances communication between you and your spouse
- Provides a time to completely relax
- Relieves stress

- Ensures continued development of your relationship over the years
- Provides moments to discuss dreams
- Facilitates problem resolution
- Ignites romance and keeps the flames burning through the busy times

Sit down together and make a list of activities you would like to do together. It may require some 'give and take' as you compile your list. For many couples, this is true even if you simply want to go to a movie. She might choose a romantic comedy while he prefers an action film. This decision will require compromise. Make sure date night does not become a battleground. You will defeat your purpose.

Date night does not have to be an evening event. If you are retired or have flexible work schedules, you may choose a date day. Or you may want to plan some date nights in your own home. If you have children this will require finding a place for your children to go. Some date nights will require money and others, maybe some of the best, will be free. Set aside some of your household budget for date night.

Date night ideas:

- Movie
- Dinner or lunch at new restaurant
- A walk in the park or neighborhood
- A candlelight dinner at home
- Visit display homes and plan your future dream house
- A night of dancing
- Rent a movie, pop popcorn, and snuggle in bed
- Window shop
- Concert in the park
- Watch a sporting event such as baseball, football, or a hockey game

- Go bowling or play miniature golf
- Boating in the park
- See a play, or go to the symphony
- Read poetry or an inspiring/romantic book together in a secluded spot
- Share a hobby

Once in a while plan a surprise date for which your partner does not know the plan. The unexpected can be pleasant surprise. My husband planned such a night. I didn't know his plans but he said to dress casual and bring a sweater. We went to a nearby park on a cool night. We snuggled on a park bench and shared what turned out to be one of the most important events in our married life. Then we went to a restaurant and shared a yummy desert. It was very romantic and I enjoyed not knowing the plans ahead of time.

Today's Refrigerator Bulletin:
   "Keep your marriage alive: date your mate!"

Family Reunion

Q: I am distressed! My life is so hectic that I am losing touch with my relatives. I desperately want to get my extended family together on a regular basis so we can watch the children grow and keep abreast of each other's lives.

A: Family reunions are an excellent vehicle for preserving family bonds. First, decide how often you want to see these relatives. Then, schedule a time to meet once a year, twice a year, or monthly. Make it a tradition everyone can plan on and look forward to attending. There is security in establishing a family reunion as a tradition because it provides a convenient time and place to maintain your feeling of connection.

You can plan a reunion anytime of the year but plan the location and activities according to the weather. In the warmer months, you can reserve a pavilion in a park or reserve a subdivision pool facility. In cold weather you will need to rent an inside facility such as a city recreational center, a subdivision country club, or space in a church or synagogue where a family member attends. If your group is small, someone's home may provide adequate space.

Suggestions for the reunion:

- The event may be elaborate from time to time, but as a general rule, make the event simple.

335

- Rotate the planning responsibilities each year so that the same person does not do all the work. You will all benefit from the ideas and expertise of others and the work will be divided. Arrange for a committee with a chairman.

- Collect money from each household to cover the expenses of the event.

- Hire a photographer to take a group picture. You may be able to negotiate an inexpensive package if the photographer knows he has the potential to sell several packages. Some may want individual shots of their immediate family taken.

- Have several people take photos of the days' events. Preserve the photos in a scrapbook so previous reunions can be enjoyed each year. Save the negatives in case others would like copies of specific pictures.

- Shoot a video of the reunion each year.

- Create entertainment with the talents in the family or hire an outsider. Provide activities for all ages such as a band, a disk jockey, a clown, a story teller, or a magician.

- Create a newsletter sharing information exclusively about the family. This could be produced monthly or once a year. Include information such as reunion news, birthdays, anniversaries, births, recognitions, and accomplishments. Each family could also include a paragraph about what is going on in their lives.

- Arrange to serve food for the event. Hire a caterer, plan a potluck, or have each family bring their own food.

- Plan games for the day such as relays, a carnival, softball, or volleyball.

- Maximize the use of everyone's careers and talents. A journalist or writer could publish the newsletter. A teacher could plan the games. A homemaker could plan the menu for the day.

Today's Refrigerator Bulletin:
'Strengthen family ties by planning family reunions!'

Small Visitors

Q: Last week, a visiting toddler broke one of my favorite knick-knacks. I want everyone to feel welcome in my home. How can I prepare for small visitors?

A: When small visitors come calling, you must consider two primary objectives: To ensure the safety of the child, and to protect significant items on display in your home. Let's talk about protecting your valuables first.   Be prepared to put breakable items away or, if you entertain toddlers often, display them on shelves that are out of reach. If you collect antiques or glassware, follow this out-of-reach rule, or store your valuables in a locked display cabinet. As a safety consideration, make sure that the furniture is stable and cannot be pulled down or overturned. You may want to secure tall shelves and display cases to the wall. 'Don't touch' and 'no' simply do not work effectively with all toddlers.

Some households will accommodate these curtain crawlers better than others. A home decorated with items such as baskets, teddy bears, needlepoint pillows, and quilts provide a relatively safe environment. Although you may not want these treasures played with, they will not break. If you are especially attached to some of these items and they cannot be laundered, cover them or take them out of harm's way. Another option is to block off areas of your home that contain more individual items than you can conveniently put away.

The amount of time you spend preparing your home for small visitors should be determined by how often they visit. Grandparents or regular baby-sitters may need some permanent accommodations. If this is the case you may want to arrange an area in your home with a portable bed, small table, chairs, toys, and books. Purchase these items inexpensively at garage sales or browse the want ads.

Be prepared to feed these visitors. Make sure you have a high chair or booster seat. This will protect the furniture in other rooms of your home from food and sticky fingers. Keep toddler cups, small silverware, and bibs on hand. Keep a supply of appropriate snacks such as crackers, animal cookies, cereal, and apple juice.

Make your home safe. Cover electrical outlets and hide electrical chords. Put up gates or close doors next to stairways. Put house pets in other rooms if they are not tolerant of young children. Make sure floors are clean and free of debris. Crawling infants taste-test everything they touch.

Purchase or rent children's videos for their entertainment. You can also record children's shows from television. Regularly check your television guide for a listing of children's shows. An alternative to television is to use a tape recorder with cassette tapes of music or stories accompanied by a book.

If your visitors come daily or weekly you may want to spend some time outside. In this case you will want a stroller, tricycle, or other small riding toy. If you no longer have these items from when your own children were small, look for a sale at a discount store, a garage sale, or have the parents bring them. Hang a baby swing from a tree branch in your backyard.

If small children visit you occasionally you will want to keep your preparations simple. Purchase a large plastic container and fill it with a few items such as, toys, books, toddler cup and silverware. Store the container on a shelf in your basement. If no high chair or booster seat is available, use your imagination to come up with a safe alternative. In any case, let the parents know ahead of time what items and supplies you have so they can plan to bring what you lack.

Since my children are older and small visitors come occasionally, I have a shelf in my basement for items I would need. There is a portable bed that fits into a duffel bag, a high chair, booster seat and plastic container filled with baby and toddler toys. In my kitchen I keep several toddler cups, silverware, and bibs. These are all items I have saved from my own children's younger years.

Today's Refrigerator Bulletin:
"Make your home safe, fun, and accommodating for small visitors!"

About the Author

Diana Koenig is a successful writer, educator, and lecturer. She has inspired thousands to become more organized and more efficient through her nationally published column, "Domestic Planner®." As a wife, homemaker, and the mother of four, she combines practical insights with tried and true techniques to help bring order to the lives of the 'organizationally challenged.' Diana is much in demand as a speaker, seminar leader, home/business consultant and is regularly featured on local television. Diana has a B.A. in Elementary Education.